HOW TO BECOME
A TOTAL FAILURE

The Ten Rules of
Highly Unsuccessful People

Success

BILL GUILLORY, PH.D. AND PHIL DAVIS

First Edition

ISBN 0-933241-19-4

Printed in the United States of America
Innovations International, Inc., Publishing Division

Designed by Tatiana A. Haynes and
Kathleen E. Di Francesco

Library of Congress Cataloging-in-Publication Data

This book is dedicated to our daughters and their success: Lea, Kayla, Candice, Alicia, Chelsea, and Shyanne.

The Rules *for* Failure

Contents

The Rules *for* Failure

Contents

Introduction

Have you ever asked yourself why it is so much easier to fail than to succeed? Success requires dedication, effort, and a willingness to continually learn. Most of the skills we learn for success and failure are typically acquired from our childhood experiences. As youngsters, we are so loaded with decisions about life that we are bound to program a few that are detrimental to our success. We define these as The Rules *for* Failure.

For example, have you ever watched children in a nursery? If a child wants a toy, he or she walks over and takes it from someone who is playing with it. Decision time! The child who was playing with the toy either takes action to retrieve it or sits there and cries; fight or flight. If crying is the choice, the child who took the toy may decide, "Whenever I want something, I simply take it." This is a variation of Rule #4: Always look out for Number One. Although this decision may appear, at the time, to be a rule for success, it eventually becomes a rule for failure.

By the time we are thirteen years old, we've just about mastered the rules we believe are essential to get what we want in life—but not necessarily the rules to ensure our success. The rules to get what we want serve as the basis for the behavioral patterns (and skills) we begin to perfect for navigating life.

The point is, we begin to learn a selective set of skills for failing fairly early in life. Every time we attempt to avoid responsibility for what we do, selfishly manipulate our parents, throw temper tantrums to get our way, and get what we want with the least amount of effort, we are establishing a pattern of behavior that will ultimately lead to failure. Having learned from experience, our parents attempt to teach us the long-term consequences of such behavioral patterns, which are not in our best interests. Sometimes, we listen and learn, and sometimes we don't.

Armed with our storehouse of wisdom, we are thrust upon the school system. Their job is to teach us the skills for success. The problem is we've already perfected many of the skills for failure! So teachers have the dual challenge of helping us unlearn our pattern of failure *and* simultaneously teaching us skills for success; such as honesty, hard work, sharing, and most of all, how to get along with others. You can understand why our school system is in such a mess today. Not primarily because of the teachers or the system but because of our dysfunctional preconditioning before we even enter the hallowed halls of learning.

The Rules *for* Failure (The Rules) are also reinforced through competition for grades, participation in cliques, and the general acceptance and glorification of antisocial behavior. The Rules appear to be such an ingrained part of life that by the time we enter the world of work we use them without a second thought. They become such a natural part of our day-to-day behaviors that we are honestly surprised when someone calls attention to the fact that gossip is injurious to others, that hoarding information undermines productivity, or resistance to new learning is the quickest way to put the organization out of business—and ourselves out of a job.

The Rules are so socially acceptable that being a proponent for success is almost a radical idea. In practice, The Rules appear to be innocent and well-meaning, but in fact they are personally self-serving, and ironically, also self-defeating. Let's get started with our examination of how The Rules are used in "real life" situations. We warn you in advance, we will use "tongue in cheek" comments to keep the conversations and the stories humorous. The ultimate objective, however, is to reassess the long-term value of The Rules *for* Failure and learn how to transform them into The Rules *for* Success. We rarely stop to consider that "failure is success in disguise."

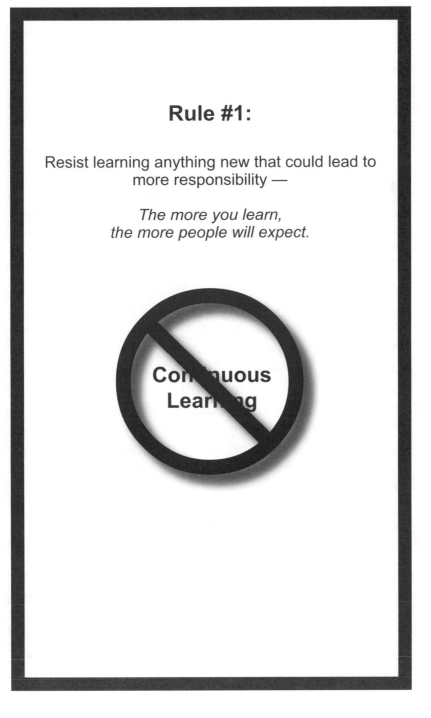

Rule #1:

Resist learning anything new that could lead to
more responsibility —

*The more you learn,
the more people will expect.*

ONE OF THE MOST COMMON EXAMPLES OF RULE #1 occurs in organizations where employees are resistant to new learning. As workplace demands increase in terms of speed, efficiency, and quality, workers feel greater pressure to do more work in less time; and to do so with less management. This is called empowerment.[1] If, in fact, workers don't learn new skills for workplace efficiency, then empowerment *does* become more work in less time. In this situation, the strategy for failure in dealing with greater workplace responsibility is Rule #1: resist new learning and create a smoke screen where empowerment itself *appears* to be the problem. Effective smoke screens include the suggestion that training takes employees away from their real work and it's simply a waste of time or that leadership is trying to get more out of workers without extra pay; which in some cases may have validity! Let's visit a few stories to learn the consequences of resisting new learning by using Rule #1.

₪

The following story was shared by a friend during her early days of managing. It involves her best effort at

[1]*Empowerment* is the ability to perform with the least amount of supervision.

running a franchise business during the rapid integration of information technology (IT). This is an excellent example of the application of Rule #1, and its rather unsuccessful resulting consequences.

E-Filing? What a Dumb Idea!

When I was first getting started in the printing business, one of my part-time employees came to me with the idea of offering e-file taxes for our customers. This was back in 1990 before the Internet age. If he had come to me a few years later, I might have been more open-minded, but I had no idea how to send documents over a phone line. "It's simple," he said, pointing to the small computer screen. "You just click this button and the computer breaks up all the data into tiny little 1s and 0s, fires them across the telephone line, and the computer on the other end reassembles the pieces into the tax return you see right here."

His whole idea sounded wishy-washy to me, too Star Trekky. I told him that we were not in the tax filing business and dismissed the idea. He persisted, saying that our customers come to us to make copies of their tax returns every year so why couldn't we help them file their forms faster? "They'll get their money faster. Don't you think people will pay for that?" "No," I said. "I think people will think we're nuts, but even if they do think we can send their tax returns over a phone line to the IRS, they won't trust us having their private information sent in some hocus pocus fashion. And I don't want to take on that responsibility. Do you?" Before he could answer, I simply continued, "You should just drop the whole idea."

Instead of dropping his idea, he drove down to our corporate headquarters in Albuquerque, New Mexico, and somehow got the CEO to listen to him. I have never been so angry in all my life and I was planning on firing him when he returned. I couldn't believe a part-time employee would have the nerve to disrespect me so blatantly. When he returned, I called him into my office. But before I could tell him he was fired, he told me the CEO wanted to test the e-filing idea in our store. "What?" I yelled. "First you go down there without my permission—after I told you to drop the whole idea— and now you want me to help you test it? Did you ever think what would happen to me if your cute little idea doesn't work?"

The guy just stood there grinning like an idiot; and his pimples didn't help. He was too naïve to understand how easy it was to lose a job and he didn't have a family he was trying to support. The bad news is we tested the idea and actually made money. The good news is a majority of the other 137 franchise partners in the organization voted to reject the service. The whole e-filing idea died a good democratic death, at least as a service provided by our company.

This story illustrates the fear we experience when new information technology (IT) and computer software have to be learned. In this case, the manager's first objection to the new idea was the responsibility she would have if something bad happened to a customer's tax information. The second reason for her opposition to the new idea was that *she* might look bad if it failed and would lose her job. These are both superficial objections that were used to hide her *real* fear—the necessity to learn the new IT competencies and skills required for implementing the new e-filing idea. The eventual consequence was that over time she lost credibility in the organization and ultimately she lost her job as a manager for being too risk-averse. Too often we let our fear of new learning, and possibly more responsibility, lead us down a road to failure.

₪

Let's take a look at what often happens on the home front when we're just learning how to master the skill of avoiding new learning and greater responsibility.

I Don't Know How to Make French Toast

A few months ago, I offered to make breakfast for my wife and four daughters. They were delighted, so I proudly prepared my breakfast specialty: fluffy scrambled eggs, crispy bacon, and wheat toast, just to add a healthy touch. One of my daughters, Angela, who marches to her own drummer, commented that she wanted French toast. I told her that it would be much easier if she had bacon and eggs. She just looked at me and stated that she had no interest in bacon and eggs. She even went on to point out that wheat bread made no healthy difference because of the grease I was using.

I finally said, "Fine! Why don't you make it yourself?" She began to whine that she didn't know how to make French toast. I tried to be funny by replying that making French toast was a survival skill that every kid should learn. She rolled her eyes, let out a resigned "Puh-lease!" and said she wasn't interested in learning, just eating. However, she did agree to put up with my cooking class. Copying the techniques of the *Emeril Live* cooking show from T.V., I walked her through the mastery process of preparing French toast, while she watched with a mildly interested look.

About this time my oldest daughter walked into the kitchen and asked what was going on. When I told her about my cooking class in French toast, she laughed and said, "What are you talking about? Angela makes French toast all the time." So much for my household heroics. Angela took the plate and muttered, "Thanks for teaching me the *new* survival skill. I'm sure it'll come in handy if I'm ever stranded in the woods."

In spite of the attitude our kids may possibly use sometimes to avoid new learning, we have to be vigilant in teaching them anyway; even when they may well be putting us on! They might not appreciate us now, but they will in the future. There's a running debate about how much we influence our children's habits and how much they are influenced by their friends. I think we are lucky if it's fifty-fifty. No matter what we expect their school to teach them, we are 100% responsible for preparing them for the world they will encounter when they grow up. We can only do so by becoming credible examples of the expectations we have of them. Remember, we influence them most by what we *do*, and to a lesser extent by what we *say*.

₪

Our concluding example involving the mastery of avoiding new learning is the story of Casey, whose job was to keep an eye on things. This job description is perfectly suited for the application of Rule #1.

My Job is To Keep an Eye on Things

I once worked as an assistant manager for a family-owned printing business. The owner, Helen, spent most of her time in an inner office. This was her idea of running an empowered operation. Helen's husband, Casey, worked customer service with a limited crew of teenage staff. The staff spent most of their time sitting around reading novels except when *interrupted* by customers during periods of high demand. Casey was a nice guy, fun to talk with during slow spells, but when the office got busy he just hung out by one of the machines talking to no one in particular. Most of the time I'm not sure he even noticed that no one was listening to him because we were too busy helping customers and running jobs. On occasion, his wife, Helen, would make an appearance just to let us know she was alive and well.

One day I finally had enough of Casey's goofing off. I didn't care if Helen fired me or not, I figured I could always drop out of college and fry burgers or something. While running three machines simultaneously and trying to politely pay attention to one of Casey's rambling stories, I stopped and asked, "Casey, would you mind running one of these jobs so I can work on the other two that have just come in?" "Sorry," he said, "I don't know how to run this machine." *Ah-ha,* I thought, *now I've got him.* "It's really easy," I replied. "Here, let me show you." "No, it's okay," Casey said, still standing with his elbow propped on the machine I wanted him to operate. "You don't need to show me." "Why not?" I asked, about ready to explode.

"Well," Casey replied, "if you teach me how to operate the machine then everyone will expect me to operate it

all the time and that's not what Helen wants me to do."
I was stunned. "What *does* Helen want you to do?" I
asked. "I'm supposed to keep an eye on things while
she's running her office," Casey said. "But she's the
only one in the office!" I almost shouted. Casey replied,
"That's exactly what I mean. She can't do everything
you know." He just stood there staring at me as if what
he had just said made perfect sense. I simply walked
away and started to make plans for a new job. While
Casey kept an eye on things, Helen sat in her office,
and the crew read their novels, our customers did a
disappearing act!

This story highlights the challenges small businesses
face in today's competitive business environment. The
fact is, small businesses are subject to the same rules of
business operation as large organizations. By comparison,
many large business franchises operate exactly like Helen
and Casey's organization. The fundamental rule for any
business—large or small—is when continuous learning
stops, extinction quickly sets in.

Conclusion

The point of each of these stories is that new learning,
one way or another, is unavoidable. After all, the most
important asset you have where work is concerned is your
competency. Competency refers to your total set of skills,
talents, and learned experiences. We refer to this asset
as your "personal stock." By comparison to the Stock
Market, the higher your personal stock, the greater value
you have. Conversely, the less competent you are, the less
value you have in the world of work. This simple analogy

shows clearly that resistance to new learning is eventually a prescription for failure. The ultimate realization for success is to adopt a mind-set that continuous learning is a requirement for continuous employment.

Rule #2:

Don't share what you know with others —

Knowledge is power;
don't give away your power.

A COMMON EXAMPLE OF RULE #2 IS COMPETITION for grades, both in high school and college. We learn fairly early not to share lecture notes with those who missed class or even homework assignments in highly competitive situations like honors courses. Given our early mastery of information hoarding, we are already prepared to put Rule #2 into practice upon entering the workplace. For example, prior to the advent of personal computers (PCs) the middle manager was considered to be the most powerful person in the information chain. He or she controlled information up and down the organization. During this period, privileged information was the most valuable commodity for power and control. Privileged information included whose budget would be cut, whose job was in jeopardy, and what new initiatives were going to be implemented, such as a reorganization. These were the "days of wine and roses" for the middle manager.

All of this changed when the PC came along and secretaries became the most powerful people in the information chain. Primarily because they had already perfected keyboarding (called typing at the time) and they were less averse to learning the new computer technology (in opposition to Rule #1).

One of the delicate dilemmas of not sharing what you know also involves coaching others. More often than not, there is a need to teach someone else the skills that you've mastered, such as a computer software program, a laboratory test procedure, or even how to do *your* job. The latter is definitely considered a red flag. Teaching someone your job is the most threatening of all; particularly if there is talk about transferring you to another division. The *other* division might be in another company.

The delicate skill in this situation is to learn how to teach a lot of detail with very little substance. When mentoring others about your job, it's vital that you hold back on the critical information that has made you indispensable. Your knowledge of your job is the most important asset you have in the workplace. It's your source of power! You must protect it at all costs—even if you fail in the long run. Let's visit a few examples that will help you sharpen your skills in retaining your power.

₪

The following story illustrates the consequences of taking information hoarding to an extreme, particularly in one's self-interest.

The Covert General Manager

I once held the position of vice president of the Asia-Pacific division for a U.S.-based machine tool company. One of my responsibilities was to forecast sales for the region each quarter. All general managers (GM) were required to send me their quarterly forecast. I would, in turn, report the forecasts to the CEO in the U.S. For two consecutive quarters, I hadn't received forecasts from our office in South Korea. For those quarters, I projected (code for "made up") numbers I thought were reasonable.

During the third quarter I became so agitated with our Seoul GM for not sending his sales forecasts, I flew out to have a heart-to-heart talk with him. Upon arriving at his office, I began to discuss his financials and what his sales forecast was for the current quarter. Before he could respond, his cell phone rang. He excused himself with a suspicious look and left the room to take the call. When he returned, he began to complain about the technical issues he was having with the factory in Taiwan, completely ignoring my earlier questions about his sales projections. I realized he was trying to avoid our conversation about having another poor quarter, but I decided to let him rant on as I've learned that sometimes it's better to let people hang *themselves*; which they usually do if you give them enough rope. I figured I'd give him as much rope as he needed to do the job and watch him slowly twist in the wind.

When he stopped to take a break from his tirade, I asked him if I could see his sales forecast. There was complete silence for a few uncomfortable moments and then he leaned over the table and whispered conspiratorially, "I can't show you my sales forecast." "Why not?" I asked, beginning to feel uncomfortable. He sat back with a thin smile and said that he couldn't discuss the details of a project he was working on because the customer was the South Korean government and they had made him sign a non-disclosure agreement (NDA). Now he was being ridiculous since any NDA would also apply to me or any other employee involved in such a project; and I told him so. In response, he became even more serious, and leaned across the table again and said to me with complete sincerity, "You don't know this, but I am an agent for the CIA." I began laughing, but he remained completely serious.

After firing him, I spent several weeks in his office sorting things out and training a new GM. One of the first things I did was to look into this "big account" the GM was supposed to be closing with the South Korean government. It turned out that the GM, whose sanity was in question, *had* been working on such a contract. I subsequently emailed him and asked him why he hadn't openly told me about the deal before my visit. He replied, "The order was so large (this one order would have been 10 times his normal annual revenue), I was afraid corporate (meaning me) would come in and take over the contract," which in turn would lower his commission rate.

He confessed to me later in a telephone conversation that his *CIA* story had not been a good idea, but it was the first thing that had popped into his mind when I pressured him to see the forecast. He ended our conversation by laughingly saying, "If I had told you about the government contract, I would have had to kill you." I didn't think his comment was very funny.

Learning to trust people with information, even people within our own organizations, can be a difficult task. However, the more we share information and knowledge with others the more buy-in and support we get. For example, the South Korean GM learned afterward that if he had been open about his huge contract with the government, his vice president would have made sure he received his full commission. In addition, his vice president would have exerted every resource at his disposal to assist the GM in being successful. Instead, the GM was fired and the company lost the contract, a lose/lose situation.

This rule is a two-way street. While hoarding information can cause a lot of damage, people need to feel that they can trust those around them before they divulge information they feel is important to their survival and success. An environment of openness and trust needs to be developed within people *as well as* the organization in order for information sharing to become a practiced reality.

₪

Hoarding information on the home front can also be a dangerous game, particularly, if the situation has implications involving the Internal Revenue Service (IRS). The following story describes a well-meaning fiscal practice that could have resulted in dire consequences for Dave and Brenda.

The Secret Fund

When Dave and Brenda were married it was decided that Brenda would manage the household money. She loved saving money and Dave loved spending it. Brenda's mother had taught her from a very early age how to manage money, and most of all to set aside some for inevitable "rainy days." The key element was that this "rainy day cache" was not to be revealed to Dave, since he would likely spend it. Dave was an independent contractor responsible for reporting his own taxable income. When Dave would occasionally ask how they were doing financially, Brenda would give him a vague answer that implied they were doing okay. This arrangement was fine with Dave as long as he was allowed to have his wide-screen TV, heavy duty pick-up truck for hauling the RV, and something extra for hanging out with his buddies to do "guy stuff."

Then one day Dave received an official letter from the IRS. This is always a bad omen. The IRS rarely writes you to ask how well you are doing financially or offer extra money for an old tax return just in case you're having hard times. The official letter indicated Dave owed $10,000 in back taxes. According to the IRS records, Dave and Brenda had not disclosed a portion of their income for several years after their marriage. When Dave asked Brenda about the IRS letter, she suggested that the IRS must have made a mistake. Dave decided to "go to war" with the IRS. He set up an appointment with the local IRS representative to "straighten out" the situation, since he had such confidence in Brenda's financial management.

When he told Brenda of his appointment, she seemed uneasy. Dave thought she would be proud of his stand since, in part, he was also defending his confidence in her ability to manage their finances. Surprisingly, Brenda suggested he cancel his appointment and pay the $10,000 back taxes. Astonished, Dave asked, "Why?" "Because it's not worth it. You know they are determined to win, no matter what the situation is," Brenda replied.

After a long silence, Dave asked, "What is it you're not telling me?" Brenda let out a long sigh and responded, "I was taught to always have a secret fund that my husband didn't know about." "What for?" he asked. "Kids, college, emergencies, or whatever!" she exclaimed, now on the verge of tears. "I was just doing what I thought was best for the family. You love to spend money. I was taught how to save it," she explained softly. "We have a savings account," Dave replied. "But you know about that," she responded. "So?" he appealed. "So if you know about it you'll eventually find a reason to spend it," she replied defiantly.

That statement hit Dave in the gut. He realized, at that moment, he hadn't really wanted to know their financial situation. He just wanted to spend money for what he fancied at the time and yet have no responsibility for checks and balances. That was Brenda's job. Her secret fund made perfect sense for someone's spouse who operated in an irresponsible way about spending. He should actually thank the IRS for creating the mini crisis they were experiencing. As these realizations downloaded in rapid succession, Dave decided he would first pay the back taxes with apologies to the Agent. Second, he would play a more honest and responsible role in their financial management. He never thought he would ever credit the IRS for eventually saving their marriage.

Money is the number one reason married couples divorce. When irresponsible spending is coupled with secret money set aside, it's a formula for disaster. Dave's realization of his reckless spending pattern was the breakthrough to establishing a new money management system in their marriage—a system based upon openness, honesty, and responsibility. The statement about money being the reason for failed marriages is not entirely accurate—people are the reason. Situations like Dave and Brenda's provide either an incredible opportunity for reinventing a marriage (or a committed relationship) or ignoring new learning, which commonly results in two people going their separate ways to run the same pattern again!

Conclusion

In spite of our heroic efforts to avoid sharing what we know with others, it appears to be a losing cause. The emphasis of practically every new technological device is the rapid and comprehensive dissemination of information, from computers to *iPods* to mobile phones to personal digital assistants. In truth, there is little we can prevent others from knowing, except perhaps our thoughts; and even hiding our thoughts from highly intuitive individuals is not guaranteed. One way or another, the truth always catches up with us. Even the major business prospectuses, such as *The McKinsey Quarterly*, discuss the power of networking in adapting to organizational change. Almost everything we do today—from business to personal activities—requires the participation and cooperation of others. We are in the Age of Collaboration. Therefore, information sharing, networking, and teaming are essential for business and family success.

It is important to understand that information and knowledge are not the same thing. Information is simply a set of interrelated facts or data, such as temperature, estimated time of arrival, strategies, and plans. Knowledge is the result of *creating* a new idea that is often transformed into a new product or service from the information you know, such as the transistor, a silicon chip, nanotechnology, or efficiently running a household. (In fact, the estimated salary for effectively and efficiently managing a household in 2008 was $140,000.)

Therefore, as stated in the introductory quote of this chapter, "knowledge is power." The point is, you never have to worry about running out of knowledge as long as you're creative. *Power is not a zero-sum game.* Power is unlimited because the creation of new knowledge is unlimited.

Rule #3:

Be a jerk! —

*Jerks get what they want because decent
behaviors are not expected.*

ONE OF THE ADVANTAGES OF BEING A *JERK*[2] IS THAT nobody wants to be around you; unless he or she absolutely has to. That means that you have lots of time alone where you can plot and scheme how to sabotage the people blocking your success. Since there's no chance of any meaningful relationships, you never have to feel guilty about what you say to people or even how you say it. They've come to accept you for the jerk that you are. An added advantage is that you never have to deal with the discomfort of people's feelings and emotions; even your own. This point is captured by the one-liner from the movie *Wall Street*, when Gordon Gekko (played by actor Michael Douglas) comments about those financially hurt by illegal insider trading, "If you want a friend, get a dog." Yes, there are definite advantages to being a jerk. Let's review a few situations to discover the short- and long-term consequences of this rule.

₪

The following story was shared verbatim by the daughter of a friend who claimed she had direct experience with two or three jerks on an annual basis.

---

[2]A jerk is a person who practices obnoxious, counterproductive, and insensitive behaviors.

The Relatives

The worst event of our family's summer vacation time is when my uncle shows up with his five children. Two of the three boys make a joke out of the phrase "antisocial behavior." They are definitely schizoid. Their idea of fun is picking their noses during meals or even telling dirty jokes. The tragedy is their parents think their antics are funny or they are just too embarrassed to correct them. *These kids are bona fide jerks.* On one occasion I asked one of them, "Why do you act the way you do?" His reply was, "That's what people expect, because they put up with it."

The most difficult part of being forced to be around them is that they don't bathe. I don't mean irregularly, I mean at all! They might visit us for a week at which point I can't wait for them to leave. Although the boys range in age from thirteen to seventeen years old, their "mastery of life" is violent video games. They have no idea of what's going on in the world and appear to have no interest. The worst part of this whole situation is that our parents pretend we actually look forward to their summer visits, when they know my sister and I hate them. After the family's last visit, word got back to their parents about our opinion of their boys. Their parents were appalled. They officially informed our parents that we would not be blessed with their visit next summer. Thank God!

One thing jerks can depend on is that sensitive, understanding behavior is totally unexpected of them. In fact, jerks assume they can get away with just about anything since correcting their behavior appears to be too much work, and *we* assume it won't make any difference anyway. We also assume life will catch up with them in some way or another for the misery they have caused others, and it usually does. So the short-term strategy we use is to avoid jerks as much as possible and then at some point rid ourselves of them permanently; except for weddings and funerals in the case of relatives. In situations like the story described above, it's really the parents' responsibility to be sensitive and understanding of their children rather than subjecting their kids to an annual ordeal to which *they* (parents) feel *obligated.*

₪

The following story is an eye-opening shared experience of a vice president for a U.S. retail chain store. It's an example of blatant ethnocentrism[3] at the expense of business success.

It's All Greek to Me

When I was vice president of a U.S.-based retail chain store in Asia-Pacific, I was assigned to assist the new general manager (GM) in finding a high-profile business location in Sydney, Australia. Although the GM had been looking for a suitable location for seven months, he reported that he had been unsuccessful. He indicated further in his correspondence that things moved at a slower pace in that part of the world as compared to the U.S. I responded that I understood the differences in time and pace, but that seven months

[3] *Ethnocentrism* is the human tendency to believe that one's own culture or value system is superior to others.

was "long" by any standards. He indicated that laying the "groundwork of relationship" was an essential part of selecting a suitable location. "After all, some types of people can be trusted more than others," he stated in a telephone conversation. I wasn't sure what he meant by that comment, but I would soon find out. I was directed by the CEO to fly to Sydney to find a location within a week in order to make a recommendation for an upcoming board meeting.

On the first day, we found a great location that was in the heart of the Sydney business district. The floor plan was perfect for our retail products. I was thinking about celebrating the rest of the week as this was my first visit to Sydney. However, the GM indicated the location was, without question, unsuitable. Incredulously, I asked, "Why?"He took me outside the hearing range of the owner and whispered, "He's Greek." I said, "What?" He moved me further away from the building and said, "You don't understand these people. They can't be trusted. If we sign a multi-year agreement, we'll have problems for the entire lease."

I still thought he was joking, but after a while it dawned on me that he was dead serious. In spite of my misgivings, I was clear that if this new entree into Australia was going to be successful, I would have to have the total commitment of the GM. So I felt forced to find another location with an owner he felt comfortable with. "She" was outstanding, but the location was clearly less desirable from a business perspective as compared to the Greek's retail space. I began to suspect why it took seven months to lay the "groundwork of relationship" for finding a suitable location.

In spite of the fact that the store did well, subsequent stores were not as successful in Sydney. The GM was phased out within two years, more because of complaints by employees about his blatant opinion of selected ethnic groups, than business performance. I'm convinced that the chosen location of the first store was critical to the subsequent lack of success of the other stores. We never did establish the market potential in Sydney, simply because the original location didn't attract the critical mass of traffic we needed for success.

What's there to say, the GM is a classic jerk. His ethnocentric attitudes about certain groups were so strong that he even allowed them to influence his business decisions. His being phased out was predictable. It was just a matter of time. Quite frankly, it's surprising that he was selected as GM in the first place!

₪

In the early days of facilitating diversity courses, if you didn't show up with a flak jacket, you were in deep trouble. You were also lucky if you had just a few participants who wanted to be there. Things have gotten considerably better since that time, but you can still anticipate there will be at least one participant who is not convinced the course is of any value. His or her job is to not only invalidate the course but engage the facilitator in a no-win confrontation. The following story illustrates this point.

Jerking Around the Facilitator

One of the most difficult courses to facilitate is diversity—probably because no one wants to discover he or she is biased or prejudiced. In my years of teaching diversity, there was one course that challenged me most. When I asked this particular group to introduce themselves, one of the participants, Perry, indicated that he was forced to attend and if he didn't like the presentation he would leave. I said okay and stated that dealing with difficult subjects such as diversity could be cathartic. He replied, "Like taking an enema?" When everyone laughed, I knew I was in trouble.

Since I love repartee, my first thought was to reply, "So that's why you've been squirming so much in your seat." My second thought was that he was scared of the course and trying to find a reason to leave through a confrontation with me. I immediately decided that we would be friends before the course was over. Throughout the morning he continued to test my patience with one-liners such as, "entitlement is the problem, not discrimination," "around here women get special treatment," or "this course is a waste of time." I simply acknowledged his comments and, most of all, his right to his opinion.

In the afternoon, the seminar participants grew progressively tired of his comments. *They* began to challenge his statements. Strong emotions began to emerge. I simply allowed the heated discussions to take place as an "innocent" observer. At one point, I thought I was going to have to save Perry from some violent group action. Visualize that picture—*me saving him!* The culminating statement was made by a female participant who stated, "Perry, you've been a stupid jerk the whole day." When the "dialogue" was complete, we had one of the best courses I had ever facilitated.

In our work, we refer to Perry as a "petty tyrant." A petty tyrant is someone who is there to teach a facilitator a whole new dimension of unconditional acceptance. And in doing so, the facilitator learns and grows to a whole new level of human understanding. Perry came up to me after everyone had left and told me a story of how a black female had been recently promoted instead of him. He thought of quitting, but he had his pension to consider. We discussed how he might take a new, proactive approach to his career and I gave him my email address for further conversations. We have since become good friends.

The most critical requirements for diversity facilitation are understanding, tolerance, and acceptance of others. A condition for these requirements is the recognition and acknowledgement that we are *all* biased and prejudiced in some way. Given this level of understanding you can recognize that Perry's behaviors were hiding a part of himself he was scared to discover and possibly reveal. The key in this situation was to allow the seminar group to participate in the process of facilitating Perry's insensitive remarks. As revealed in this story, obnoxious, counterproductive, and insensitive behaviors run their course in the short term and become the reasons for failure (and new learning) in the long term.

Conclusion

The point of the stories in this chapter is that being a jerk may have short-term advantages, but more often than not, such conduct will catch up with you in the long term. These behaviors are often used to hide interpersonal insecurities. By taking a non-judgmental approach to such an individual, the opportunity for resolution of the individual's issue will soon present itself. Playing along or reacting negatively are the behaviors that keep his or her insecurities in place. Good managerial supervision, skilled facilitation, or parental understanding in the case of "The Relatives" is the most appropriate solution.

Rule #4:

Always look out for Number One! —

It's a zero-sum game.

THIS RULE IS AN ABSOLUTE MUST IN AN INDIVIDUALISTIC society, like the United States, or anywhere in the Western world. Like former football coach Henry "Red" Sanders said, "Winning isn't everything, it's the *only* thing." And the winners are those who have mastered the skill of looking out for themselves.

Now what exactly do we mean by looking out for Number One? We mean the same thing that Darwin proposed 150 years ago—*survival of the fittest*. One of the first instructions given on airline flights is to put on *your* oxygen mask first, and then help someone else—that is, if it's convenient. The flight attendants also ask if you are willing to help others if you sit in an emergency exit row seat. Most of us say "yes," but I suspect our unspoken thought is, *I'm out of here first and will help others from the exterior of the plane*. This is not selfishness. This is a natural law for all human beings. How can you possibly help someone else—if that's your thing—if you haven't helped yourself first? After all, we learn very early in life that "the Lord helps those who help themselves *first*!"

Some years ago, a friend of ours, Phil, went on a vacation with his significant other, Karen, to one of the Caribbean Islands. After hanging out on the beach most of the day drinking "Yellow Birds" (spiced with 151 Bacardi rum), they decided to take a dip in the cool Atlantic waters. They were feeling no pain and experiencing an expanded state of consciousness. In fact, it took supreme effort to simply make a trip to the bathroom. They talked about their soul connection and how they were committed to each other for all of time and eternity. Then, out of the blue Karen suggested they swim out to the island. The island was a strip of land about a hundred yards offshore (about the length of a football field). Besides feeling no pain, Phil had "Bird Power." So with a smile he replied, "Let's go for it, Babe." Karen was a strong swimmer and had raced competitively in high school. Phil was a "natural athlete" by his own designation—a legend in his own mind. If Karen could make it, so could he.

They fearlessly began their quest for the island. He "allowed" Karen to swim ahead of him, just in case she got into trouble. After all, it was his responsibility to protect her; particularly, since they were bonded for life. When the distance between them started to lengthen, Phil realized his "Bird Power" was gone. Then a cold, strong undercurrent began to pull them farther from the island. They had not seen it from shore. All Phil could see was "pure Atlantic blue" and 3,000 miles to Europe! He started to get an ominous feeling in his stomach as the island seemed to get farther away than when they had started. It's called fear.

The next thought Phil had was, *you're in trouble boy!* The other part of his mind said, *don't sweat it, you're a natural athlete.* Phil looked for Karen to make sure she was okay. All he could see was her strong, high school kick. He shouted out to her, "Karen, I think I'm in trouble. I don't know if I can make it!" She looked back at him, her eyes as big as saucers, then turned and continued to haul ass for the island. So much for their soul connection.

It was then that Phil realized that it was all about looking out for himself. His own instinct for survival kicked in (or his Guardian Angel came to his rescue) and he felt stronger than ever. When they reached the island and got their bearings, they simply looked at each other for a long time. Something had irrevocably changed about their relationship. When they returned home, they eventually drifted apart and went their separate ways.

This story raises an interesting question. Are there times when "looking out for Number One" is justified, or are these times a test of a deeper human instinct? A situation like this provides an opportunity for each of us to learn something about ourselves that goes *beyond* always looking out for Number One—even when our own survival may be threatened.

ᆈ

As the saying goes, the most important lessons in life are learned through personal experiences, or more precisely, through experiences of failure. The ones that have the greatest impact are those that involve lost opportunities with significant monetary implications. Such situations have the greatest potential for personal transformation and enlightenment. The following story is an example of this experience.

One Hundred Percent of Nothing!

I have a close friend in the consulting business. He runs a one-man show from a virtual office. His virtual office includes his home, the airport, tennis courts, restaurants, and most of all, his car. Since he has no physical office, he runs a paperless operation. Everything is done using information technology.

On one occasion, he misplaced his BlackBerry, which is the *source* of his independent style of operation. He immediately went into a state of shock and paralysis. His wife was trying to get him more involved in the family, so she hid it. When she explained the joke, he seriously considered filing for divorce. Unfortunately, he couldn't do that since she was such a valuable source of new leads for his business. A few days after the "incident" of the misplaced BlackBerry, his wife informed him of a contractual opportunity that equaled his six-month income. His first thought was, *should I bring in others or go it alone and subcontract as needed*? That was a no-brainer, he chose going it alone; while visions of $$$$$ danced in his head.

When he made the short list of the final three consulting firms in competition for the contract, he was asked to give three reference organizations his firm had served for a contract of that size. Blank. There were none he had served alone, so he was eliminated from consideration. Losing that contract reminded him of the phrase a good friend had told him, "Fifty percent of something is better than 100 percent of nothing!" Something snapped. He had a moment of enlightenment.

Three weeks later he was contacted by an old friend with whom he had worked in a previous job. She needed a comprehensive change management program in her organization that required extensive consulting resources. He immediately called a colleague whose organization had everything he needed. They formed a partnership that provided outstanding service for his friend's company. Even more important, they created a formal strategic partnership to market, sell, serve, and develop new breakthrough products and services.

In spite of our focus on Number One, in business and life, it's a collaborative world. Sometimes technology gives us the illusion we can go it alone and still be successful, but sooner or later, we discover that working collaboratively with others is the key to sustained success. At a deeper level, collaboration is the acknowledgment that we are inherently connected. Unfortunately for many, if not most of us, it takes a crisis to discover that connection.

₪

When we are young, carefree, and talented we can easily become self-centered. People around us, including our parents, begin to treat us like we are special—in the sense of making excuses for our shortcomings, allowing us to cheat and get by, and most of all acting as though we are better than they are. Our talent and their worship of "heroes" feed our egos into getting practically anything we want, until someone comes along and destroys the illusion. When this situation *inevitably* occurs, we discover that we are no better than anyone else. This is a humbling but growth-producing experience as described by Barry's Story.

Barry's Story

Barry not only looked out for Number One most of his life, but most people treated him like Number One. He was a typical "golden boy," six feet, four inches tall and charismatic. He was a high school quarterback phenomenon who was heavily recruited by most of the major football universities. His parents were middle class, working people who would mortgage their home to give Barry anything he wanted; and Barry wanted a lot. When he turned sixteen, he asked for and received a new sports car for his birthday. When he wanted to attend an expensive football camp during the summer, somehow his parents found a way to pay for it by taking on extra work.

Unfortunately, academic achievement was not high on Barry's list of priorities, so he learned how to "finesse" his way through high school. That is, he either copied other classmates' homework or cheated on exams. He had a dedicated following that was all too happy to aid and abet this seemingly minor requirement for success. After leading his high school football team to its second state championship, Barry entered one of the most prestigious football programs in the U.S. Unfortunately for Barry, this program was equally serious about its scholastic program.

Barry was shocked. They actually expected him to attend all of his classes *and* personally earn passing grades. It was then he realized how inadequate and frightened he felt about his inability to meet the academic requirements on his own. His first thought was to revert to his tried-and-true method of operation (MO)—use his fan club. However, it was clear that the athletic program had no intention of being subjected to NCAA sanctions for grade-fixing. Meanwhile, on the athletic front he was being equally challenged.

When the starting quarterback was injured in a crucial game, Barry was chosen to replace him. On several of their possessions, Barry changed the plays sent in by the coach to favor his own personal involvement. When confronted by the coach, Barry told him that the plays he changed were necessary for the team to succeed. The coach replied, "You don't seem to understand, Son. It's not about you. It's about the team."

Barry had heard all that "team talk" over and over again in high school but when the game was on the line it was really all about him. After all, that's why they recruited him in the first place, he reasoned. The coach thought for a moment and then emphatically told Barry that he was out of the game and benched until he learned the "team concept." Barry was stunned, devastated, and decidedly angry. Without football and the stardom that came with it, why was he here? What about his dream to become a National Football League (NFL) quarterback? After being benched, his life became a downward spiral resulting in a state of depression. He had come face-to-face with his basic life principle—"look out for Number One."

To simply give up that driving force of his life was exposing himself to a vulnerability that he had not experienced since childhood. Given his family's financial status, he had learned early in life that he had to look out for himself. The best way to do so was to *use* his God-given athletic talent in his own self-interest. Unfortunately, that strategy was not working in his present situation. The choices he was facing were change or fail! It was as simple as that. Needless to say, this was Barry's "moment of truth."

At the completion of his process of introspection he felt as though a new personality had taken over his body. He saw, felt, and experienced the world differently. His soul-searching began by recounting all the people he had *used* for his own selfish purposes, particularly, his parents. He experienced a deep sense of shame, guilt, and remorse. He decided he couldn't change the past, but he could begin anew by how he treated people in the future. His most important realization was that he was really never Number One when he considered all the people who had played crucial roles in his success; such as his parents, friends, schoolmates, teammates, teachers, coaches, fans, etc. This realization turned his life around and ultimately led to his success as part of an athletic distribution business when he finished college.

ﭑ

Although Barry is the major character in this story, those who aided and abetted his "look out for Number One" attitude along the way contributed measurably to his MO. We often pretend to be innocent of how we play "enabling" roles in someone else's pattern of behavior that is insensitive to the roles of others. Fortunately, the university football coach provided the confrontation necessary for Barry to come face-to-face with his ego-driven pattern of using others for his personal success. The good news is that Barry chose to deal with his insensitive, behavioral pattern rather than continue down a path with possibly greater injurious consequences to himself and others.

Conclusion

Sooner or later, most of us just "get it." *Always looking out for Number One* in an increasingly complex world just won't sustain our personal or professional success. We find ourselves resorting to more manipulation, scheming, and cutting our losses. In addition, winning alone starts to feel empty. We have all the gold, but no one to share it with who experienced the journey with us. At the end of this process of introspection, we discover it's all about collaboration rather than competition. Particularly, when competition breeds a Number One mentality at the expense of others.

In today's interconnected world, it's even hard to *define* Number One; let alone look out for him or her. Whether it's sports, business, or our personal lives, there always seems to be others involved in most things we do. So we have a double precaution when thinking only of Number One. First, there are very few things we can do alone and gain satisfaction from. Second, if we try to take total credit for a cooperative effort, the other part of the "cooperative" will probably be resentful.

Setting aside the consequences of looking out for Number One, there is a greater awareness we might discover. That is, we are all talented in some unique way. That unique talent makes us all Number One. It's simply a matter of discovering what we are Number One at and living it full out!

Rule #5:

It's all about the money —

Money equals success.

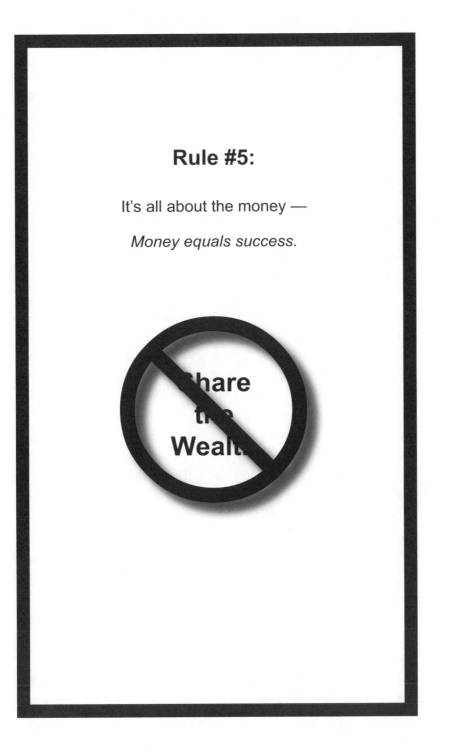

N O MATTER HOW MUCH WE TALK ABOUT QUALITY OF life in the U.S., the standard for success is how much money you *have*, not simply how much you earn. To illustrate this point, two movies immediately come to mind: *Jerry Maguire* and *Wall Street*. The character, Jerry Maguire, is a professional sports agent who will do just about anything to get the biggest contract for his clients, plus a generous commission for himself. Then one day he has an epiphany and is fired for expressing it. His epiphany leads him to write a mission statement that advocates *better service, fewer clients,* and *less focus* on *money*. Ironically, he ends up with one remaining client who is an egomaniacal football player whose favorite line to Jerry is "Show me the money!" In the end, they both ended up with money *and* a quality relationship. As we said, it's a movie. In real life, you rarely get both. So what's the message in reality? *Go for the Money*!

Wall Street is the story of a young stockbroker, Bud Fox, who is desperate to get to the top. He is successful in getting a wealthy corporate raider, Gordon Gekko, as his mentor. Bud learns that Gekko's success is due to acquiring insider information, but chooses to partner with him anyway. After a short span of financial success beyond his wildest imagination, Bud Fox is indicted for insider trading. The indictment precipitates a moment of truth for Bud when he learns that Gekko plans to do a corporate raid on his father's company, Bluestar Airlines.

Gekko's statements to the Bluestar stockholders during their annual meeting captures the essence of this rule in action: "Greed is good. Greed is right. Greed works. Greed clarifies, cuts through, and captures the essence of the evolutionary spirit." Bud must choose between the rich insider's lifestyle offered by breaking the law or his father's values of hard work and fair play. In the end, he chooses the latter. As we said previously, it's a movie. Bud did have a great spin, because he got the girl and the money, albeit for the short term. In Bud's case, "it's better to have been rich and lost than to have never been rich at all." Right?

Putting movies aside, our real-life folk heroes today are celebrities such as Warren Buffett, CEO of Berkshire Hathaway (one of the world's most successful investors); Bill Gates, magnate of the computing industry and one of the richest persons in the world; and Oprah Winfrey, wealthy television host who is involved in a variety of entertainment businesses. These individuals are icons of success, primarily because of the money they have earned.

Notice, for example, how the popular television program about rich people combine two terms: *Lifestyles of the Rich and Famous*. Get it? The *rich* and the *famous*. The implication is they are famous because they are rich. Setting aside the *non-rich* and *famous* for the moment, such as Mother Teresa, Martin Luther King, and Mohandas Gandhi, for most of us, deep down, money equals success. Let's review a few stories to help crystallize the point we're making.

₪

The following story illustrates the kind of attitude you need to have if you plan to be a serious player in the game of life. You must have a "hunter attitude." You have to be a predator. Save feelings and emotions for your personal relationships or your pets. In business, particularly sales, you eat what you kill.

You Eat What You Kill

Several years ago, one of our clients attempted to establish a team approach to selling to their customers. This approach was based on the assumption that a team could win a greater volume of sales than each individual operating alone. A member of the sales force, Gil, felt that this new approach was designed to undermine his exceptional individual sales success and help the poor sales representatives who were simply too touchy-feely to close deals. Gil's mantra was "You eat what you kill." His response to team selling was that if the others didn't understand the hard realities of sales they ought to get a job in marketing where no accountability for sales is expected.

Gil was a loner and proud of it. He was a survivor. He was smooth talking and promised clients whatever they requested. His travel expenses included everything from a four-mile drive to the airport to a shoe-shine to look sharp for clients. When his organization decided to seriously pursue team-selling, Gil took a job with a competing firm which fit his philosophy perfectly. After a year with this new firm, his sales results did not meet his quota. In this new environment, everyone was a predator. When Gil asked for a six-month extension of his base pay, his sales manager smiled and said, "Gil, in this firm, you eat what you kill. If you don't kill anything how do you expect to eat?" Last I heard Gil was working as a security guard for a K-Mart store.

It would appear in Gil's situation that if you operate as though life is jungle survival, then that's the reality you get. I guess there is some validity to the belief that what you put out in the way you live your life is exactly what you get back in terms of how life treats you. Like Bud Fox, Gil was a short-term success story, but in the long run he was more like a falling star.

₪

The following story illustrates when it's all about the money, particularly when you are using other people's money—namely your organization's. This is a story of true mastery of ensuring your monetary success, before and after the fact!

If You Want To Get Fired, Buy a Golf Course!

A friend of mine, Justin Weber, was headhunted from an Asian competitor to help U.S.-based Tidewater Corporation "clean house" in their Japanese office. The CEO of Tidewater informed Justin that the company was having a problem with their Japanese operations. He was specifically concerned about the financial management of the current president of the Japanese subsidiary, Scott Becker. When Justin arrived in Japan, his first task was to evaluate the performance of the current president, particularly with respect to the spending of unrestricted funds. Well, if spending hundreds, if not thousands, of dollars several nights a week in expensive Japanese nightclubs as well as drinking and flirting with beautiful women were good financial management, then the current president was doing a bang-up job.

When confronted, Scott attempted to explain to Justin that in Japan everything was based on relationship. "You mean spending company money in expensive night clubs?" Justin asked. Scott responded, "You didn't expect me to use my own money for cross-cultural learning did you? I thought I was doing the company a favor by putting in time *after* regular business hours." "Did you get any new business?" Justin inquired. "These things take time. But I did establish a few very 'promising leads,'" the president responded with a chuckle and a wink. Justin replied with a stony expression, "That's not exactly what I had in mind." Unfortunately for the president, Justin determined that his nightly escapades were not only unsound financial management but also did little to add value to the company's bottom line.

The crowning blow came when Justin discovered that the president had purchased a $100,000 share in his favorite golfing country club; an investment that was now worth about $10,000. Needless to say, the CEO back in the U.S. was not happy to hear this news and the president was immediately relieved of his duties. Justin was promoted to replace him just weeks after arriving in Tokyo. Upon assuming his new presidential duties, Justin learned that the former president's name could not be taken off the golf club membership because Tidewater would have to absorb a $90,000 loss. Since the CEO didn't want his investors or Wall Street to learn of the golf membership fiasco, the organization gave the membership to the ex-president as part of his severance package. He might not have the income to support his former night life, but he's got one hell of a place to go take a shower when he needs one.

The point of this story is that all too often senior executives let the money and the perks of their positions corrupt their ethical judgment. You don't have to watch *CNN Headline News* very often to hear another story of an executive going to jail for the misuse of corporate funds. Remember Enron and World Comm? In 2007, Paul Wolfowitz, head of the World Bank, was forced to resign. His resignation involved excessive pay given to an employee based upon their personal relationship.

"Money is the root of all evil," so the saying goes. Perhaps, what we *do* with money based upon our ethical judgment is a more accurate description of this statement. Allowing money to lead us down the slippery slope of compromised ethics or corruption will ensure failure in the short term and possible imprisonment in the long term!

₪

The final story illustrating Rule #5, is about a multinational corporation that was successful in running highly profitable businesses throughout the world. The executives were happy. The shareholders were happy. The employees, however, were overworked, dissatisfied and stressed: a time bomb in the making. The following story explains why, as well as what happened to the time bomb.

Old Dogs Can Learn New Tricks

Buford Brown was an "Executive Specialist" for the multinational corporation, Global Services International (GSI). He was affectionately known as "Buster Brown," and not because of the shoes he wore. He specialized in transforming profit-losing businesses into profit-making operations. His major arsenal of tools consisted of down-sizing, eliminating profit-losing activities, and control and command management. Buster was generously compensated for the extraordinary turn-around times he achieved in several business operations. As the Age of Empowerment began to seriously emerge, Buster became less of an asset and more of a liability. In other words, he was becoming expendable. The days of being hailed as a hero on the cover of national magazines because of getting rid of people to become profitable were fast disappearing. Particularly, when the remaining employees had to handle the same amount of work that existed before downsizing.

Buster was assigned to one of GSI's West European operations that was continually breaking even. At GSI, breaking even didn't cut it. Upon his arrival at the European site he met with Judy Kern, the second in command. Judy was a no-nonsense, straight-forward manager. Buster began outlining his usual "plan for profitability." Judy responded, "That plan won't work here." "Why not?" Buster asked. Judy replied, "That's the kind of leadership and management we've had for the last five years." When Buster hesitated, Judy continued, "What do you think will happen to you if the situation gets worse here?" It didn't take Buster very long to figure out the answer to that question. Furthermore, if his superiors knew in advance the situation Judy described, why was he sent?

After a sleepless night, Buster met Judy the following morning to plan his strategy. He asked her what she thought might work? "Greater empowerment" was her answer. *What a novel idea*, he thought, sarcastically. "What exactly does that mean?" he inquired. "It means respect, delegation in proportion to competency, and the development of our people," Judy said. Buster responded, "That's going to take time and cost us money!" "It's your call," she said, sitting back to wait for his response.

Buster realized that he was out of his element—both in terms of a profitability strategy, as well as a second in command as confident as Judy. He knew his only strategy was to create profitability on whatever terms his work force responded to best, and that appeared to be empowerment. Fear-based management simply wasn't as successful anymore, particularly, with the influx of Gen X and Y employees. This was a "moment of truth" for Buster because he also realized that his only hope for success was Judy. So he asked her, "Would you help me make this work?" Judy responded, "Only if I have the final say on critical decisions."

Buster realized for the first time what it meant to have no control and still have ultimate accountability. However, in spite of this "double bubble," he had no choice. Little did he realize that Judy was not a gamble.

She not only knew how to implement empowerment, but she also had the confidence and support of the work force. Over the next two years, the European operation set the standard for the next generation's global operation of GSI. Buster retired and Judy Kern became the new Executive Specialist in the global incorporation of empowerment.

The moral of this story is that empowerment and profitability are not mutually exclusive. In fact, they are a mutual necessity in today's fast-paced world of business. The basic premise of empowerment is that positively motivated people will perform better in the short and long term as compared to fear-driven performance which is indicative of "command and control." Buster's signature mode of operation had simply run its course. Success and profitability in the present business world require continuously learning, knowledgeable employees who work together in collaboration and comprehensively share information.

Conclusion

The question that naturally arises is, what distinguishes the Gordon Gekkos, Bud Foxes, and Gils of the world from our icons Warren Buffett, Bill Gates, and Oprah Winfrey? The first difference would appear to be staying power— not only how much money they earn but also how much they retain. The second difference is what they have done in behalf of societal good.

In June 2007, Warren Buffett announced he had irrevocably earmarked the majority of his Berkshire

Hathaway shares to charity. At the time, the gift was worth $31 billion, believed to be the largest gift in history. It will go primarily to the Bill and Melinda Gates Foundation.

It is well documented that the Bill and Melinda Gates Foundation has been one of the largest single donors in the world to global health, poverty and hunger, and technology education for America's most vulnerable populations. The Gateses have focused their time and talents on tackling such diseases as hepatitis, AIDS, and malaria in Africa, increasing the graduation rate of America's cultural and ethnic minorities, and helping women abroad start small businesses.

Oprah Winfrey established a Leadership Academy for Girls in South Africa. She has also made considerable contributions to education for the underprivileged as well as publishing and film for the betterment of humankind. Perhaps, the guiding principle for her contribution to societal good is captured by her quote from the *Good Housekeeping* magazine on integrity, "Real integrity is doing the right thing, knowing that nobody's going to know whether you did it or not."

The point is, what distinguishes these individuals, and *many others*, who have accumulated large sums of money, is that it's **not** all about them or the money. It's about the welfare of humankind.

We would be remiss if we didn't add a postscript about the opposite of this rule. That is to acknowledge the millions of those who share what they have on a day-to-day basis who have not accumulated large sums of money. In the final analysis, it's not about the "size of the pot"— money accumulated—but the size of the heart in sharing whatever the pot is with others.

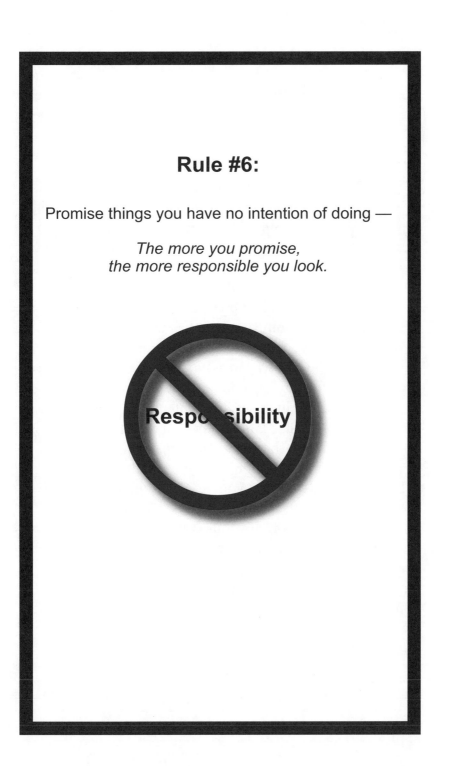

HAVE YOU EVER THOUGHT ABOUT THE NUMBER OF promises you make on a daily or weekly basis? For example, if you meet a friend you haven't seen in months or even years, you promise to give him or her a call to set a date for lunch or a drink, when you know you have absolutely no intention of doing so. And you don't! Why? It takes time, energy, and effort, particularly, with someone who has not recently been on your radar screen. Somehow, we feel guilty about the long absence and the best way to assuage our guilt is to promise some form of follow-up contact.

The key word in this rule is "intention." This is a very powerful word, since more often than not, it is a reflection of what ultimately happens. How many times have you said to someone, "I didn't intend for that to happen." However, whatever it is you are denying is exactly what repeatedly occurs!

Things get more serious when promises involve workplace situations. If promises, intentions, and results are not aligned, the consequences are typically loss of one's job, opportunity, or customers. When we begin to equate intention with results, then we can avoid disappointments and ultimately severed relationships.

ﬡ

The problem with workplace and business promises is that people expect them to be done. They expect you to not only be responsible but also accountable for what you promised. The following story is a perfect example of promises made, promises broken, and a permanently severed friendship.

Promises, Promises

A good friend of mine, Craig, established a contractual agreement with an old college buddy, Dennis. Dennis is bright, outgoing and has an infectious personality. Everybody loves him. Dennis promised to provide the information technology (IT) needed for Craig's budding Internet marketing business. Craig paid Dennis half in advance since their relationship was based on years of trust.

At first, Craig overlooked the missed deadlines to customers because Dennis didn't deliver the backend IT he needed. Dennis sent an email to Craig to inform him that "everything was cool" and that he was working on an IT design that would "knock the socks" off of Craig's customers. Although Craig was doubtful of Dennis' reliability, he recalled their college days together and their close friendship. On reflection, he also recalled that their friendship in college was based on parties, shooting the breeze, and chasing co-eds. These reflections were good reason for anxiety where his business was concerned.

A week before a major appointment, Craig had not received Dennis' program for presentation to a major prospective customer. In fact, Craig learned through the grapevine that Dennis had returned to his native

Mediterranean home to "soak in some rays," without a word to Craig. He also learned that several of his college friends who had IT deals with Dennis were also disappointed by Dennis' unannounced disappearance. Fortunately, Craig found another source for his IT needs and launched a very successful and profitable Internet marketing venture. Dennis returned after a year's absence and informed Craig that he was back in town and available to help take Craig's business to the next level. Craig did not reply. Dennis was dumbfounded.

The point of this story is self-evident. If you ask someone to fulfill a business responsibility and he or she agrees, and then proceeds to violate that promise, you are in trouble. "What you see is what you get." Furthermore, you don't need a succession of missed promises. If it happens "once," it's a pattern! Like the wisdom saying of the ages, "Action speaks louder than words." Sometimes sabotage is even unconscious to the person doing it. However, he or she quickly regains consciousness when asked to move on.

נ

One of the most important promises we make and break quite easily is the marriage vow. We promise to separate only when "death do us part." Yet, the present divorce rate in the U.S. is somewhere between 50 and 60 percent of all first marriages. The following story sheds some light on why divorce happens to many of us—through self-discovery *after* marriage.

The Game of LIFE®

When Monica Merchant first met Jerry Bradshaw it was love at first sight. They partied. They travelled. They worked with passion. They were stone Buppies (Black Urban Professionals). The obvious "event" after a year of "personal discovery" was jumping the broom (marriage). Next, they bought an upwardly-mobile crib in the burbs. As they surveyed the game board called LIFE®, they decided it was time to experiment with the team process of creating a family. After all, you're not quite sure everything works until pregnancy results in the delivery of an offspring. They were so delighted with their first creation, Jennifer, and the fun they had doing it, that they decided to go for it two more times in quick succession. This is when reality began to set in. Big time. Jerry was still on the fast track as Monica assumed most of the child-rearing duties. He would promise to be home for family dinner, but office emergencies often prevented him from doing so.

At five years old, Jennifer showed a natural talent for the violin. She began participating in recitals around the city. Jerry rarely showed up for her performances after endless promises. Finally, Monica confronted him using the soft approach. "Jerry, Jennifer is truly disappointed when you don't show up for her recitals," Monica pointed out in a caring manner. Jerry replied, "Well since you're there the family is covered." "The family is not covered," she responded with increased emotion. "Baby, I'm just trying to bring home the bread," he replied. "You're too self-centered is the problem," Monica retorted. "All you care about is your work and your friends." Recognizing the seriousness of her tone,

Jerry raised both hands, palms up and said, "You're right. I promise to come to Jennifer's recitals and be home for family dinner from now on." Monica was happy, but wary about his promise.

Over the next six months, Jerry was careful not to make promises he could not keep; which amounted to about half the events Monica expected. She hoped things would get better with time. However, as time went on, Monica began to notice that "making promises and breaking them" was a pattern in Jerry's behavior, depending on the activities that were truly important to him. Whenever something came up that involved sports, his friends, or his career, everything else got pushed aside or ignored.

The marriage breaker occurred when he missed Jennifer's graduation recital. His absence involved an emergency meeting with an out-of-town client critical to his business portfolio. When he came home late that evening, he approached Monica in a contrite manner. "Hey baby, I'm sorry, but I just couldn't blow off my most important client." She replied, "But you could blow off the most important performance of your daughter's life." He responded somewhat angrily, "There will be other recitals!" "Not with us, there won't!" she snapped back. "What do you mean?" he asked. "We simply don't have the same values," she said in a resigned tone. "I think that it is best if we went our separate ways. Nothing is more important to me than family—no matter what the emergency might be. It's as simple as that."

Jerry realized for the first time that he valued his family, but not at the expense of his professional aspirations in life. He also realized that his pattern of prioritizing his promises was the source of this realization. If Monica's strongly held opinion was "family or nothing" then he realized their marriage would not work. So they divorced without retribution or anger. Oddly enough, he began attending more of Jennifer's recitals than before they were divorced.

Reconciling family responsibilities and professional aspirations is probably the most challenging dilemma we face in the early part of our careers. Unfortunately, most of us don't consciously think about family values as a basis for marriage. Our primary focus is commonly on our mutual compatibility with a partner. We learn about the other aspects of family *after* we're in a marital (or committed) relationship. That's when "growing up" really begins. And a lot of growing up requires rethinking, deprogramming, and reprogramming patterns of failure that we have adopted. Whether it's personal or professional, a critical pattern for success in life is "Promises made are promises kept."

₪

The following story is about a five-year old promise made by a father to his seven-year-old daughter. The promise that started out as a charade culminated in a defining moment for both daughter and father.

Horsing Around

One of my biggest problems in being a Dad is making promises to my children. After all, I don't want them to think we can't afford stuff like their rich friends, even if we can't. So when my seven-year-old daughter, Jennifer, asked for a horse for her birthday, I told her I would buy her one when she turned twelve. I figured I'd be rich by then. I had just left the company I had been with for ten years with considerable entrepreneurial experience in starting new businesses around the world—albeit using their money. However, I also figured that Jennifer would forget about a horse by age twelve and I'd begin dealing with more serious requests, such as parties and dates with BOYS!

She didn't forget on her eighth birthday, her ninth birthday, or her tenth birthday. As the years rolled by, my wife began to enlighten me regarding the cost of a horse and the expenses to keep and tend one—beginning with a lovely country home. I'd always fantasized about being a country squire ever since growing up on our family ranch in Wyoming. When Jennifer turned eleven years-old, her enthusiasm began to soar about the horse she would have and how she would ride it every day. In a like manner, my spirits started to plummet as I began to figure out how I was going to tell Jennifer that a horse wasn't in her horoscope. This admission not only involved dashing Jennifer's five-year dream but also the three other kids' confidence in me as a father "who keeps his promises." In truth, my promise was unrealistic.

As I prepared to tell the truth to Jennifer, I felt progressively worse because the other kids got caught up in her excitement. I finally decided to "bite the bullet" and own up to my five-year charade. "Hey Jen, we need to talk over some things; just me and you," I said with a serious look on my face. Her eyes brightened, her smile broadened, and her look of anticipation was clearly obvious. "Sure, Daddy, let's talk." She stopped abruptly and said, "Just a minute," and she took off. When she returned she had a worn and battered catalog of Western accessories with saddles, bridles, clothing, and so on. She said, "I'm ready, Daddy." I was momentarily stopped. After she followed me into the living room and we were alone, I asked her to sit down. She looked directly into my eyes expectantly.

I began, "I know how much you've looked forward to owning your own horse since you were seven years old." Her smile dimmed just a bit. I continued, "The cost of a horse is quite expensive and the upkeep for a year is even more." Her smile was totally gone by now and I thought I could just see the beginning of tears in the corners of her eyes. I went on, "So what I would like to propose is we share the rental of a horse every week with two other young kids just like you. In fact, you can get to know each other and feed the horse together. Then someone else can take care of the horse. It'll be just like yours except we won't own it. The horse won't know the difference." Her smile began to slowly return. She jumped up and hugged me tighter than ever before. Then she released a torrent of tears. And so did I. This was one promise I had guaranteed in advance. In retrospect, my stock as a father reached an all time high at that time.

Experience has taught us that promises made to children carry a life-long impact. Promises are also critical in shaping parent-child relationships, particularly with respect to fathers and daughters. There's not much to say about this situation that isn't implicit except, "keep your word" and "don't promise what you can't deliver" where your children are concerned. Remember, these are their "wonder years." Lots of decisions are being made about men by daughters, and fathers are in the starring role.

Conclusion

The focus of this rule is a lack of personal responsibility. If you find yourself practicing this rule it is likely that others will view you as unreliable and less credible; particularly those you care about most. If you practice this rule in the workplace, then you are forcing your supervisor to hold you responsible for your job. If you are a supervisor who is unwilling to hold others responsible for the expectations associated with their jobs, then you ought to take a less responsible position.

Supervising is less about being liked or being popular than it is about ensuring the performance necessary to keep the organization in business. Good supervising equally involves understanding, compassion, and respect for people. These two dimensions of supervising performance and people are not mutually exclusive. The ideal situation would be where each person holds himself or herself responsible without the necessity of being supervised— which is called self-management.

Rule #7:

It's always someone else's fault —

Success is dependent on your ability to CYA!

Accou tability

I F YOU SERIOUSLY CONSIDER THE NATURE OF PEOPLE IN THIS world, this rule is probably true most of the time. A friend of ours works as the assistant to an executive vice president. On a recent occasion, the vice president was rushing to the airport for an important meeting and asked her to get the phone number of the client he was meeting in another city. She went to their database program, wrote down the number, and wished him well for his meeting. After discovering his flight was delayed, he dialed the number she gave him and learned it was his client's previous number from a location four years ago. When he called his office, he was informed that his assistant had left for the day.

He finally made contact with his client when his plane arrived. Although he apologized profusely, his client was very upset and threatened to discontinue their contractural agreement. When he returned from his trip, he related to his assistant the difficulty he had in contacting the client.

She asked him bluntly, "Are you suggesting the wrong number was my fault?"

He replied, "Of course! Don't you think so?"

"No," she answered, "that's the number in the database program. *Someone* should have updated it. After all, you were in a rush so I did the best I could in the time I had. You ought to thank me for how quickly I got the number for you!" And on and on she went attempting to prove the breakdown wasn't her fault.

You see what we mean by the nature of people in this world. He didn't even appreciate what she did by saying "thanks" in such a pressured situation. He actually *expected* her to know that the number was an area code in the previous location of the client. His expectations only became more unreasonable after that. So what's the solution in such situations? You have to call upon the skills you learned when dealing with the unreasonable expectations of your parents when you were growing up—CYA. The way to survive situations like this is to master the skill of "covering yourself" and show that the other person is at fault—or at the very least, it is a system's breakdown. *Both* individuals in this story seemed to have mastered this rule.

₪

The following story is simultaneously funny and serious. Funny because it shows how a three-year-old can "work" her father at such an early age. Serious because you wonder whether her ability to use Rule #7 will only improve into adolescence and adulthood. At which point, her behavioral pattern will no longer be amusing, but a skill for failure.

Emily's Story

My three-year-old, Emily, has already developed a pattern of behavior where nothing is ever her fault. I have no idea where she learned it. The only explanation is she was born with an innate ability to blame her conflicts on anyone else but herself. God forbid that "I" had anything to do with it. One day her older sister came running to me crying saying that Emily had just broken her favorite pen. She held up the two pieces to show me, which took everything I had to keep from laughing. After all, this was a serious conflict which required my parental wisdom.

I called Emily into the room. "Why did you break Heather's pen?" I asked, using my serious parental demeanor. "I didn't," she said calmly. "You did too!" shouted Heather. I told Heather to be quiet and let me, the wise grown-up, deal with Emily. "If you didn't break the pen, then who did?" I asked. "Sophie chewed it," she lied easily. Sophie is our Golden Retriever who commonly chews on anything she can get into her mouth. Emily figured Sophie would be an easy scapegoat since she couldn't say anything in her defense. How a three-year old knows to blame a dog is in itself an interesting topic for a child psychologist to figure out.

"I don't see any teeth marks," I said. "Well, she did," was Emily's reply. "But Sophie was outside when this happened," I said, thinking I had trapped her into finally telling the truth. Emily was nonplussed. "The pen just broke," she said changing her story as if I wouldn't notice. "But you said Sophie chewed it," I said to her. "But you just said Sophie was outside," she said raising her hands up and cocking her head to the side as if I was stupid.

I sensed that I was hopelessly involved in a losing argument, but I pushed on. "How could the pen just break all by itself?" I asked, becoming more direct. She simply shrugged and said, "I don't know." "Pens don't just break for no reason," I said. "Well, it did," she insisted. "Emily, you broke Heather's pen. So say you're sorry," I said, beginning to lose my temper. "I didn't break it! It just broke!" she screamed and stormed out of the room crying. *What a great tactic*, I thought. When you run out of other people, or things, to blame, just leave the room crying. Heather stood there looking at me as if I was the dumbest Dad in the world and I felt as though she was probably right.

This wasn't the first time he had had this kind of encounter with Emily. In fact, it's difficult to remember the last time she was willing to admit to doing something wrong. He was both madder than hell and proud of the fact that he might be raising a future politician. In the Introduction of this book, we said that The Rules *for* Failure are something we learn as children. Emily is a three-year-old with three teenage siblings. While some of her behavior would appear to be innate, a human condition ingrained in her DNA, it's also quite possible she learned to mimic the behaviors of her older sisters.

How often do people we know take responsibility for their actions? Very infrequently, and yet when a person admits to a mistake, the confession is usually met with forgiveness and respect. Forgiveness because we know how difficult it is to admit to a wrongdoing and respect because we know how hard it is to be accountable for our actions and not try to cover ourselves.

₪

Although covering ourselves is probably a global rule, there are times when it is not easily excused. This is particularly true when it violates one the most important universal rules of business: "preserving face." Preserving face means making sure that you don't publicly embarrass others in the course of a business transaction, or any human situation in life.

Understanding Time and Face

After working for two years to establish a business relationship with a Japanese firm, two Americans, Jack and Jill, flew to Japan to negotiate a partnership. Dinner was planned for the first night of their arrival at 7:00 p.m. After their arrival, the two Americans slept for four hours and then spent time going over their strategy for the partnership. Jack was responsible for scheduling the activities and setting the agenda for the three-day visit. Jill was responsible for leading negotiation discussions. Jack informed Jill that the dinner was at 7:00 p.m.

When they arrived at the restaurant, their Japanese counterparts were retrieving their autos from valet parking. Jill flashed a questioning look at Jack. Their Japanese hosts were visibly upset because they had been there for dinner at 6:00 p.m. Jill prevailed upon them to at least return to the restaurant to have an after dinner drink. Their hosts agreed.

In spite of Jack and Jill's apologies, the after-dinner-drink environment was very frigid—and not because of the air conditioning. Jack then proceeded to show his hosts the emailed agenda with the 7:00 p.m. dinner agreement. One of the Japanese hosts was highly embarrassed, presumably because he was responsible for the logistics on the Japanese end. The dinner ended shortly thereafter. Although they did some business initially, the partnership eventually dissolved over time.

Proving you are right, even when you are right, very rarely wins the day, particularly if you are not aware of the protocol involving "preserving face" in most societies of the world. In this situation, Jack proved he was right about the time they were scheduled to have dinner but was inappropriate about embarrassing his hosts by proving they were wrong. Public embarrassment of someone in the Japanese culture (or most cultures of the world) is called "losing face." The person who is wrong not only loses credibility but sometimes chooses to leave that job because of the public humiliation he or she experiences.

₪

The following story was shared by a close friend who worked at a manufacturing firm in the Midwest. It's a classic case study of CYA and the resulting consequences—even when you're in a no-win situation.

The Fall Guy

Tom Larkin, vice president, was summoned to his New York corporate headquarters to answer questions regarding the subsidiary's poor quality performance. Tom chose instead to send his junior executive, Baylor Thompson, in his place. Tom said to Baylor, "You are closer to what's happening on the shop floor, so I thought you might be able to answer their questions better than me." Baylor immediately felt he was being set up as the "fall guy" to take the blame at corporate, so he made sure to take a few copies of the "tapes" along.

The corporate president, Jimmy Winthrop, greeted Baylor very cordially and asked, "What's going on in Ohio? We've pumped money into the operation and the quality defects of our products continue to increase." Baylor began to feel uneasy about where this "Inquisition" was going, but he had no intention of taking the blame. The matter was complicated by the fact that his boss, Tom Larkin, had told him before leaving, "I'm expecting you to make us look good, Baylor." Then Tom laughed and jokingly said, "Your job depends on it." Baylor didn't think this comment was so amusing.

When the corporate president started to become noticeably upset by Baylor's evasive responses, Baylor finally stated that he felt quality defects were up because of the surveillance program. "What surveillance program?" asked Jimmy. Baylor responded, "Well, sir, the surveillance program Mr. Larkin decided we needed to monitor the "real-time" performance of the workers. Mr. Larkin fully intended to let the workers know they were being monitored." "Are you serious?" Jimmy asked. Baylor responded, "I kinda suspect the workers found out about the tapes and that's when performance started to seriously deteriorate." Jimmy was becoming visibly unglued, but managed to say, "Do you realize what can happen to me, I mean to us?"

Baylor was finally feeling more relaxed than ever during the Inquisition and decided he would probably not have to use the tapes after all. He stated, "I'm sure Mr. Larkin would be happy to give you the details of the program." In spite of his participation in the program, Baylor felt he had covered himself. When he returned to the Ohio plant, he discovered that he and Tom

Larkin, and several other executives having knowledge of the surveillance program were all awarded pink slips and were immediately available for other professional opportunities.

Sometimes life presents no-win situations. In spite of the fact that a situation may be no-win, it does not mean that one is free of accountability. Covering yourself might, on the surface, appear to be in the "W" column (win), but the "A" column (accountability) is inescapable, as well as the consequences that come with it. Baylor's "pink slip" is evidence of this consequence of accountability. What's the message? CYA may work in the short term, but accountability will inevitably catch you in the long term.

Conclusion

Covering ourselves is a skill we learn by the time we can talk. According to the three-year-old in Emily's story, she has yet to do anything wrong. Our politicians are also great teachers in the art of CYA. But while CYA may let you keep your job—at least temporarily—it's a dangerous game to play because if something goes wrong, you might just find yourself in Baylor's position in *The Fall Guy* story. You might be able to fool people in the short term, but eventually people figure out the truth in the long term. I'm sure most of us have personal experiences of this rule. It's practically impossible to go through life without using it at one time or another.

Rule #8:

Truth is in the mind of the beholder —

The truth is what benefits you most.

D O YOU EVER STOP TO THINK HOW OFTEN WE LIE to each other on a daily basis? It seems that not telling the truth is a natural part of human existence. For example, when someone close to you asks your opinion of a clothing choice that you feel does not enhance their looks, what do you say? "It looks great!" Because you know that's what they want to hear. Or, someone asks you to do a task you hate that you feel obligated to do. You probably say "okay" as if you don't mind. When in truth you feel burdened and possibly taken advantage of. These are called "white" lies.

The tricky part of truth telling is when it involves deeply unconscious beliefs that can't be accurately measured. Examples include your opinion of people you dislike, the productive contribution of a coworker, or even your opinion of yourself. These are all instances where the truth is more likely in the mind of the beholder— particularly your opinion of yourself. You can begin to see that successfully navigating the workplace and life in general, requires the mastery of "personalized truth-telling." More often than not, it's the truth that we believe about ourselves that we want others to believe, particularly when it involves our self-perception or keeping a job.

ℼ

The following story illustrates how using both lying and truth-telling can be used as a technique for navigating conflicts in life. It's a perfect example of the point we made in the Introduction about learning The Rules *for* Failure as children.

The Truth Will Set You Free

Ever since Jerry was a young kid growing up in Southern California, he knew how to work the system. He was attractive, popular, and got along with everyone because of his laid-back personality. During his childhood, his parents were the system. Whenever he would get into trouble, instead of lying, Jerry's mode of operation (MO) would be to tell the truth—more or less. Then he would look contrite and promise to never do it again. It worked like magic, even through his teen years in high school, as well as in his personal relationships. Now as he entered the world of work as an account manager for a pharmaceutical company in Los Angeles, his major objective was to maintain his work-life balance; a defining characteristic of Generation Y. That meant sales in the morning and early afternoon, and surfing in the late afternoon. While other working stiffs suffered the traffic jam on Interstate 405, Jerry was "riding the waves and soaking the rays."

Jerry had inherited a stable sales route with automatic year-to-year growth, so he never bothered nurturing new sales leads. Two or three of his late afternoon clients called to complain to the sales manager, Bruce Gent, of Jerry's absence in updating their drug requests. Bruce immediately called Jerry's cell phone and repeatedly got a voice mail message.

Three hours later, Jerry returned Bruce's call. Bruce asked, "Where the hell have you been, Jerry?" Jerry responded, "My cell was off and I have been stuck in traffic on the 405. However, I did get a call in to Mr. Carver about updating their monthly drug request. Everything is cool, Mr. B." "That's interesting because I just got off the phone with Rob Carver. He said he hasn't seen or heard from you in several weeks," Bruce responded sternly. *Busted*, Jerry thought.

Then Jerry's tried-and-true MO automatically kicked into action. "Look Mr. Gent, I've been going through some personal problems that have required my attention in the late afternoons. So the truth is, I have missed some of my client calls recently. I'm honestly sorry sir, and I promise I'll make it up to them, even if I have to work until 6:00 p.m." Bruce replied, "I understand, son. Let's get together first thing tomorrow morning to work out your future direction." When Jerry met with Bruce the next morning, Bruce gave Jerry a severance check and wished him good luck in the future. He assured Jerry he would not say anything negative about him to any future employer. The Truth—more or less—had set Jerry free.

The question for Jerry is, will he decide to seriously give up his MO or continue to work it someplace else? We tend to get comfortable with our MOs, particularly if they've worked most of our lives. One failure is usually not enough to make a major life-changing decision. If so, next time all Jerry needs is a more efficient communications system for both his clients and his boss, but his work-life program is still the best around.

Sooner or later, Jerry or anyone of us who runs a "manipulative" truth-telling pattern will be confronted by someone like Jerry's boss, Bruce. It all depends on how traumatic the situation will have to be in order for each of us to give up our "old familiar ways."

ℵ

The second and most common example of personalized truth-telling is talking about others in uncomplimentary ways. This process is often described as gossip. In the following story, the direct impact of gossip is examined as well as its subsequent influence on others.

She Said, He Said, They Said!

I had a close friend named Wendy. She was very social and outgoing. Most people who knew her enjoyed her wit and easy conversation. The problem I had with Wendy was how much she talked about the shortcomings and problems of other people, even her close friends. At first I paid little attention to her comments, such as "so-and-so is a loser," "so-and-so is having marital problems," or "so-and-so has children who are out of control." The last one stopped me cold, since she could have been describing her own children. On the other hand, most of the stories she told were quite amusing. Like whose wife used vacations to get cosmetic surgery; whose husband was probably using sex-enhancing drugs; and most of all what a jerk she had for a boss.

Then I went to a seminar on relationships and communication. We did an exercise on the subject of gossip. The exercise identified three people as participants in the process: the one who gossips; the one who listens to the gossip; and the one who "innocently" overhears the gossip. (The two latter participants usually repeat what they heard to others.) Then it was suggested that the underlying intent of gossip was to undermine the reputation of the person gossiped about. It was further suggested that the two individuals who repeat what they heard were equally as guilty as the person who gossips. I was stunned by this realization. I had always considered myself to be an innocent listener who put up with Wendy's stories about others because of how much I valued our friendship. I suspected that if I confronted Wendy, I would be history as her friend. Given my realization from the seminar, I began to wonder if she also gossiped about me to others we knew.

In spite of my misgivings about what might happen in our relationship, I shared with Wendy how uncomfortable I felt when she talked about the confidential affairs of others. I was right. She was irate and told me she would never tell me anything important again. "I just don't feel right about discussing other people's personal affairs," I explained. "When did you become so righteous?" was her reply. "I'm not," I admitted. "I just saw Randy after you told me about his money problems and the repossessing of his car. He was embarrassed that I knew and so was I. He asked me how I knew about his private business and I said I couldn't tell him. Now I think I've lost him as a friend." Wendy's reply was, "Don't blame me. You've loved all my inside information until now. Besides, what we talk about has no effect on others. It's just us talking. But if you feel that way, consider yourself out of the loop. Permanently!" Wendy and I haven't talked as good friends since that incident. I miss our conversations, but not the constant gossip about others.

The funny thing about gossip is that we think we're simply relaying factual information about others. There are two problems with this assumption. The first is, more often than not, when we talk about others we are expressing a personal opinion. A personal opinion of someone is not the truth. The second problem is when we do relate a factual event (like someone's financial problems) the information is usually delivered in a negative way. That is, we usually have less respect for the person gossiped about. This is what is meant by undermining their reputation. Quite often, the revelation is that we are just as guilty by listening as my friend relaying the confidential information.

₪

Probably the most undermining form of personalized truth-telling is when it's about ourselves. More specifically, when it involves the beliefs, attitudes, and opinions we have about others that we firmly believe to be true, particularly where racial, cultural, and religious differences are concerned. The following story describes how programmed beliefs we learn as children translate into personalized truths we have as adults. When such truths are brought to conscious awareness, we are provided an opportunity to examine their validity and experience resolution where conflict is present. The transformation of Terry Cummings illustrates this process.

The Transformation of Terry Cummings

Terry Cummings first met Herb Smith at a small business seminar series. After the series ended Herb suggested they meet once a week for breakfast to exchange ideas about running their respective businesses. Terry was apprehensive about this idea since he felt it could lead to a relationship where interpersonal issues might surface. Terry believed that Herb was not the type of person with whom he could have a close, personal relationship. Although he liked Herb and continued to have occasional conversations with him, he just felt uncomfortable about interpersonal stuff becoming a part of their friendship.

When Herb's business began declining he called Terry and told him he really needed to talk with him. "I'm really over my head with travel and special projects," Terry explained. "I understand what you are saying," Herb replied. "But I'm dealing with alligators in the swamp, man, and the alligators are winning," he mused. "Can you call any of your other buddies?" Terry asked. "I guess I could, but I feel you could help me most," Herb insisted. Silence on the other end of the line.

"So what's the deal, Terry?" Herb asked. "Nothing, it's just that I'm over my head in projects," Terry repeated again. "I don't believe that's the case here," Herb responded. "Is it something personal?" Terry began to move from irritation to low-level anger. He was tired of hoping that Herb would just "get it." Subtlety was not working or Herb was simply unwilling to accept a polite "no." *What's with this white boy?* Terry asked himself as he began to recall his experience of growing up as an African-American in the South.

He had never forgotten how one of his closest childhood friendships changed dramatically when his white "friend for life," Josh, turned ten years old. For some unexplained reason, his and Josh's worlds were permanently separated. And although he had seen Josh from time-to-time, Josh never acknowledged their past friendship. As these thoughts began to emerge from his subconscious, the one that had the greatest impact was, "You can't trust white boys. They only want to use you for what they can get and move on!" *Wow*, Terry thought, where did that come from?

Meanwhile, Herb was still waiting for Terry's reply to his question. Terry said, "Hey man, I just had a thought that hit me hard. Can I call you back tomorrow?" Sensing something significant was going on with Terry, Herb asked, "Why don't we meet somewhere now and get this cleared up?" Terry's heart began pounding even harder as he experienced greater apprehension about such a meeting. He realized that this was a "moment of truth" for him. This was not the first time he had been confronted with moving a relationship with a white male to a non-superficial level. Herb asked again, "So, what's it going to be? I really need your help and I trust your judgment." The word "trust" triggered Terry's decision to meet Herb.

When they met, Herb asked again, "So what's the deal? I know it's not about business." Terry responded, "Simply put, I discovered I have deeply held beliefs about white guys from growing up as a kid. If I allow myself to have a close relationship with you, I might discover that my beliefs are not true." "So what?" Herb asked, confused as to why Terry was making such a big deal of this issue.

"So what?" Terry shouted. "Do you realize how many business opportunities I've passed up, based on my suspicions of white guys? That's not counting how many friendships I've avoided. And all along I never really knew the reason for the apprehension and suspicions I had." After what seemed like an eternity of silence between the two, Herb jokingly asked, "So are you going to get rid of me too?" They smiled with a light openness that was new to their friendship. A line had been irrevocably crossed by Terry and a bond of authentic friendship had been permanently established.

This story is a perfect example of the "workshop of life." The most powerful opportunities for transformation are life experiences where deeply held beliefs are surfaced and re-examined for their validity. For Terry, his belief about white males, as a group, was a personalized truth programmed during his childhood. In the world of business, it was also a prescription for failure in a diverse, multicultural world. When faced with his "moment of truth," Terry was willing to acknowledge his belief as a prejudice having no validity as applied to a group. This was a truth that had really set him free.

Conclusion

We all have personalized truths that we have programmed as children. The test of whether or not these truths are valid is based upon an honest evaluation of the results they have produced in our lives. If the results have been peace, harmony, and mutual benefit for us and others, then such truths are valid. If the results have been conflict, dissension, and mutual dissatisfaction then such truths are not valid. Our willingness to engage this exploration and evaluation process is the key to transforming a Rule *for* Failure into a competency for success. Go for it!

Rule #9:

Do the least that's necessary for success —

Be *all you can be but* **do** *as little as possible.*

THIS RULE REQUIRES MASTERY OF HUMAN NATURE IF you're going to do the least that's necessary *and* still be successful. For example, if you apply it to your present employment it means that you have to have a sufficient understanding of your boss or supervisor to make it difficult for him or her to fire you. This difficulty, from your boss' perspective, may be an emotional attachment such as a close personal friendship, supporting someone through a difficult personal crisis, or simply a feeling of responsibility for an employee's financial needs. So you have to make sure that your boss or supervisor is someone who is sensitive to the personal needs of his or her employees. (If you have a boss or supervisor who is heartless then you're in trouble.)

With this understanding in place, mastery of this rule involves finding your boss' weakness and using the best way to manipulate it. For example, if you're honestly going through a personal crisis and using the crisis to keep your job, then continual drama is necessary. It's also necessary for the drama to make you a victim so your boss feels sorry for you. Once your boss feels sorry for you, then anytime something goes wrong it's because of what you're going through.

However, you must also do just enough things right so that you don't get fired. This is a tricky balancing act, but I'm confident you can make it work with a little thought and practice. If you work for a heartless S.O.B., as I mentioned previously, then I suggest you go to www.jobs.com. They will help you find an endless array of new jobs that should last you a lifetime. They thrive on continually dissatisfied employees.

Better Late than Never

I have a good friend whose job it is to save the U.S. public education system. His name is Jonathan Goodfellow. No one told Jon that the education system is on life support and is in its final days of existence in its present form. As his name implies, he's not the kind of person who wants to hear bad news, which brings me to the point of this story. One of Jon's personal commitments is to transform inner city public school performance to make sure "no child is left behind." No one is quite sure what they are left behind of, but clarification is expected any day from the Department of Education in Washington, D.C.

Being the good fellow he is, Jon is having a difficult time holding his lead guy, Will Hawkins, accountable for poor results in the inner city program. Although Will puts in extraordinary hours for the project, he is in the middle of a messy divorce and splits his time between the project and going bankrupt. Jon has decided to take a whole new approach to the project that exceeds Will's qualifications. Jon informs Will that he will be reassigned as a result of the new approach. Will is shocked (or he pretends to be shocked). He reminds Jon of the long hours and sacrifices he's made for the program. Will's final appeal to Jon is a reminder of his years of commitment.

Jon wavers but sticks with his decision. Then Will becomes angry and resigns as a result of Jon's decision. Jon provides three months' severance pay to Will as a result of his dedicated service. Jon also realizes that he should have taken this action a year earlier with or without the change in the program approach. Most of all, he learned that ignoring performance as the basis for employment was compromising the cornerstone for which a manager is accountable. Without holding true to this fundamental principle of operation, it's a disservice to everyone involved, as well as those served by the project.

In a performance-oriented world, sooner or later marginal performance changes into poor performance. Unfortunately, change always creates greater expectations and a more efficient system of operation. You can run but you can't hide. In this case, Jon enabled the disablement of Will. Although Will pretended to be shocked, he was also well aware that his performance wasn't achieving expectations. Jon was so invested in being a good fellow, that he accepted marginal performance from Will for an entire year. As a last resort, he "created" a whole new approach to the project as a diplomatic way of getting rid of Will, albeit, with a generous severance package. At least Will is now free to work on his personal life transition and quality of life.

רּ

You might remember we mentioned earlier that most, if not all, of The Rules *for* Failure are learned early in life. I have a friend who has two daughters. One, Leila, is highly responsible and self-disciplined and the other, Michelle, experiences and interprets the world through her personal lens—and behaves accordingly. One of Michelle's operating principles is "How can I do the least and still achieve success?" Her mother is not quite sure when she adopted this operating principle or how, but it requires continual guidance, patience, and disciplining Michelle—often with marginal results. The following story illustrates this continuing saga between Michelle and her mother, Lori.

Life's Lessons Are Best Taught by Life Itself

After returning from school, Michelle strapped on her iPod, adjusted her sun shades, and headed for the back porch lounge chair to soak in some late afternoon rays. She also had her cell phone at arm's length for updated information exchange about the people who counted. Her mother, Lori, had other plans. She approached Michelle with the kindness of "mother's milk" and said sweetly, "Honey, after you've rested a bit, I suggest you clean up your bedroom." Michelle replied, "Why should I clean my bedroom, it's just going to get messy again?"

Lori was momentarily stopped. Then she replied, "Because we have company coming over this evening and I would like the house looking nice." Michelle simply replied, "I'll close my bedroom door." Lori's emotional barometer started to rise. Keeping her cool, she said, "There's always the possibility you might go in and out and the door is left open. It would just be nice to have everyone's room clean and tidy. Leila has already begun cleaning her room." Lori wanted to say,

"Look, I'm your mother and I said 'do it!'" However, this approach had never worked with Michelle. She simply became more defiant. With a resigned expression as though it took all of her will power, Michelle finally said, "Okay." Her body language indicated, "This is the final favor I'm granting you today."

Within five minutes she announced that her bedroom was done. When Lori went to inspect it, the bed was made haphazardly, cosmetics were still on the dresser, and everything that had been on the floor was out of sight. So Lori opened the closet to find half the stuff on the closet floor, and she found the remainder underneath the bed. By this time, Michelle had scooped up all the cosmetics and dumped them into the top drawer of the dresser. Lori suggested that she order things neatly in the closet. Michelle asked "Why? I know where everything is." Somehow, Lori realized that she had been here before with Michelle.

This was the same pattern she used with doing homework or earning school grades. "Do the minimum necessary to get by," which was nowhere near Michelle's potential. Lori began to wonder if this was a lesson that life would have to teach Michelle by failing to get something she really wanted—even when the minimum requirements were achieved. This was the first time it dawned on her that maybe some of life's lessons are best taught by life itself and not by parents.

Obviously, trying to convert Michelle through parental discipline is a losing battle. On one hand, it's our responsibility as parents to teach our children values and principles for success in life and on the other hand we all know that experience is the greatest teacher. In spite of our efforts to protect them from the bumps and bruises of life, experience is the only way some will really learn.

Most importantly, our job is to be there with love, understanding, and support no matter what the learning experiences may be. Perhaps the best motivation for love, understanding, and support is to reflect on the stupid things *we* did as children. We've found that the most essential element in influencing our children is continually working on the quality of relationship we have with them. In the final analysis, love conquers all!

₪

The following story was shared by a woman on a flight across the country. It's a story about Bob, a person who tries to do the least amount of work to get by. This is a story of change, transformation, and adaptation.

What About Bob?

Maria Sanchez works as an airline maintenance engineer. Her job is to give a thorough cleaning of airplanes after a full day's run to several U.S. cities. Her supervisor, Bob Holloway, has been with the airline for more than fifteen years. Bob's seen more trash on airplanes than most of us can accumulate in a lifetime, some speakable and some unspeakable. His most interesting caches were discovered before 9/11 when the red-eye flights were similar to night clubs. These were fondly referred to as the "champagne runs" because of the free champagne cooperative stewardesses used to give to "selected passengers." Today, Bob is occasionally treated with an iPod or

CD player that has been left behind and unclaimed. Maria takes the time to make sure every seat pouch is thoroughly emptied and all debris is removed from and around the seats. Bob has done this job for so long that his time per plane section has steadily decreased over the years to half of when he first started. On the other hand, Maria's time per section has steadily remained at twice that of Bob's.

Maria's efficiency has recently begun to annoy Bob since his work has come under increasing scrutiny. So he decided to approach Maria about an acceptable level of efficiency. "Hey, Maria, you've brought a whole new level of dedication to the team. I was wondering, for the benefit of the team, if you might speed up your time," he asked with a wide grin. She smiled in return and said, "It's not about time, Bob. It's about doing things right. Isn't that what you expect as a supervisor?"

Bob was becoming noticeably annoyed by her innocent, rah-rah answers. At that point he stated bluntly, "Just try to finish when everyone else does. No one will notice a little extra dust here and there!" "But you will. You're the supervisor," she replied with great enthusiasm. Bob concluded that the more he talked to her the more he was convinced "nobody was home." He wondered if it was a "cultural thing." Maybe he could use one of the other team members to turn on the light bulb in Maria's head. Nah, he thought, *it's my job to work this out.*

So Bob went to the maintenance manager, Harley, whom he had known for years and asked him if Maria could be reassigned to a different maintenance crew. Harley replied, "We were actually thinking about having her replace you, Bob." "What?" Bob replied, turning progressively pink in the face. "The real question is whether she'll want to keep YOU as part of the crew," Harley stated bluntly. Harley was a straight-forward no nonsense guy whom Bob tried to avoid whenever possible.

"I've been with this organization for more than fifteen years," Bob exclaimed, with an increased heart rate. "I deserve better than this, Harley." "We simply can't afford to get by anymore with haphazard maintenance, Bob. Our new strategy is based upon exceptional customer service," Harley explained. "The competition in our industry is fierce and making a profit is a whole new ball game. Given how you've performed over the last few years, I think you're lucky just to have a job in this organization," Harley concluded.

When Maria took over as the new supervisor, her first decision was to ask Bob to partner with her in making the team a success. She realized he had years of experience that was valuable. Bob felt caught in the throes of change which left him two choices—remain and change or leave and find something new.

This situation between Bob and Maria is becoming more common every day in the world of work, where a younger, ambitious worker moves rather quickly into a managerial role over more senior employees. Setting aside work ethic as a necessity, the other issue in this scenario involves generational differences between Maria and Bob. The best scenario in such cases is where the experience of a senior person can be combined with the imaginative ideas and enthusiasm of a younger person. This combination can be formidable if they compatibly integrate their differences in generation, culture, gender, work ethic, experience, and values. All of these elements are naturally involved in establishing a constructive working relationship across generations.

Conclusion

The central theme of all the stories in this chapter is that attempting to succeed by doing the least that's necessary is a losing strategy in the long run; even if you think you are achieving success in the short term. You will eventually find yourself in a vulnerable position with respect to success or continuing employment. As we stated with respect to Rule #7 (It's always someone else's fault"), we are accountable for anything that we produce in life. The earlier we adopt this way of thinking and teach it to our children, mostly by example, the more they will experience success in their own lives.

Rule #10:

The customer is someone you
have to put up with —

*Customers are never satisfied
no matter what you do.*

Cu tomer
Ser ce

W<small>E DON'T KNOW WHETHER YOU'VE NOTICED</small> or not, but in the last ten years or so customers are beginning to act like they're really special. Fortunately, there are still "bastions of sanity." For example, at the greasy diner in our neighborhood, the ancient waitress, Rosy, still tells customers, "If you don't like our coffee, go someplace else where they use real beans." The regulars get a real kick out of her comments. Most of them lost their taste buds years ago.

This whole movement started with "customer satisfaction," then "customer focus," and now it's "customer integration." We really have no interest in "integrating" with customers anyway. It sounds too "touchy-feely." In truth, we really don't like some of them. Some are demanding, impolite, and unappreciative even when you go out of your way for them. In fact, they "expect" you to go out of your way for them!

₪

The attitude that bothers us most is when customers think they know more about what's best for them than the provider. After all, the provider is the expert! Duh! The following story is an excellent example of this point.

I Want "Easy Tabs"

Very early in my career of running a small seminar business, I had the ideal customer. Their business comprised 60 percent of our income. I had a personal relationship with the CEO, and they paid us one-third in advance for our services. That was better than ideal. As you might expect, all ideal situations turn into reality (like relationships). Reality began when the organization's contact person wanted to change the wording of the training manual. I tried to explain to him that the definitions and verbiage were very carefully crafted. His comment was, "What good is that if nobody understands them?" "Then we need better educated participants," was my reply. He looked at me like I was crazy. Reflecting on the one-third payment in advance, I said, "You know, you're absolutely right. Three syllable words have a tendency to confuse people. I think I'll work on simplifying the verbiage." He smiled and expressed how grateful he was. Now that's the kind of customer I can appreciate.

About a month later, he called to ask if we could redesign the training manual. I asked him what exactly did he have in mind. He said, "It would be nice if we could have *easy tabs*." Restraining my impatience, I asked him politely, "What's an easy tab?" He said, "A tab that makes it easy to separate and locate sections of the training manual." I replied that I thought it was a great idea, but that the tabs would be sticking outside of the beautifully crafted manual. He said, "Well, the idea actually came from a majority of the participants, who are my internal customers." Now I understood the problem. Customers! I decided this was the last straw.

I had to take a stand somewhere, and this was the place. The next thing I knew he started inquiring about our Train-the-Trainer program, which turned out to be the first step in getting rid of us as a provider! As the saying goes, "You can't please all the customers all the time."

This is the classic example where a provider thinks he or she knows more about the needs of a customer than the customer himself or herself. This attitude is the "kiss of death" if you already have a customer and an attitude that will prevent you from getting any new ones. The most fundamental rule of business is *the customer knows what's best for his or her business*, regardless of how expert we might think we are. (This rule holds equally well for internal customers as well as external ones.) Even if a customer's decision is a step backwards, that's what he, she, or they need at that time. Our job is to make them successful regardless of the choices they make!

ⅎ

We have a friend who works as a sales associate for a major clothing chain. They cater to high-end, relatively wealthy clientele. The following narrative is a story she related about a new sales associate, Nancy, who didn't quite "get it" where dealing with difficult customers was concerned.

The Crabby Old Lady in Disguise

Nancy joined the sales force of a highly prestigious clothing chain. She had recently graduated from college with a degree in business administration. She brought a level of commitment and excitement to her work that the clothing chain admired in its sales associates. During one of the morning shifts, she noticed an elderly lady who appeared to be uncertain about the various clothing selections. Nancy approached her and asked with a beautiful smile, "May I help you find something?" The elderly lady looked at Nancy with disdain and replied, "I don't think so. You look like you need help more than I do." Nancy's smile disappeared and a look of indignation replaced it. Her first thought was she had never met anyone as rude as this elderly lady. Furthermore, it was unnecessary for her to be so insulting. This instant response did not escape notice by the elderly lady. Nancy recovered quickly and flashed the million-dollar smile she was taught in sales training. She replied with an air of detachment, "Well, if I can be of assistance to you, please let me know."

The elderly lady continued to pick up merchandise and carelessly throw them aside. She looked up and summoned Nancy with her eyes. When Nancy approached, the elderly lady asked, "Why is your clothing so expensive?" Nancy replied, "Because we only sell the best fabrics that will wear well for many years." The lady responded, "Will this blouse with part cotton and part acrylic shrink when washed? If so, how many sizes?" Nancy was not quite sure, so she said, "Give me a moment to ask my manager?" The elderly lady said, "Don't you know?"

Nancy replied, "I just recently started and I want to make sure I give you the right information." "Why did they hire you if you have to ask about everything I need to know?" the elderly lady asked sharply. Nancy realized she was being tested to her wit's end, and tried unsuccessfully to retain her million-dollar smile. In spite of her enthusiasm, she realized that abusive customers were not something she enjoyed putting up with. Returning to consciousness, she replied to the elderly lady, "I'll just be a minute getting the information about the blouse." By this time, the elderly lady was out of hearing range and walking to another department.

Nancy walked over to another sales associate and shared how rude she felt the elderly lady was. The other sales associate indicated that the elderly lady worked for the clothing chain. Her job was to "test" sales associates' attitudes and performance, particularly with respect to difficult customers. By mutual agreement, Nancy was reassigned to an office position within the chain. She discovered she did not have the "personal detachment" necessary to effectively deal with difficult customers.

The critical point of this story is that it is not the job of a sales person to judge and evaluate a customer. The sales person's job is to sell them something. Personal detachment is the realization that a customer's attitude has little or nothing to do with a sales person—particularly after experiencing a customer for ten seconds. As Sonny or Michael Corleone, from the movie *The Godfather,* would say, "Don't take it personal, it's just business." Sales people have volunteered, by profession, to experience every personality type and mood on the planet. Therefore, the key element for success is the mastery of human nature—which is really the mastery of one's self.

₪

The following story illustrates the well-known saying about serving customers, "Customer service is tested most during a crisis, not when things are going well." The test is usually about the quality and authenticity of the relationship between provider and customer.

My Word Is My Bond

Frank Reynolds is owner of a small machine company. He recently bought a production level water-jet cutter to keep pace with the rapid growth of his business. The sales person, Keith Jefferies, promised Frank that the new cutter could handle the increased workload Frank anticipated. This sale was critical to Keith's achieving his quota for the year. In order to ensure the sale, Keith allowed Frank to use the new model free for three months as part of the sales agreement. When Frank insisted on a signed agreement that began *after* the three-month trial period, Keith suggested that they had known each other long enough to know that "his word was his bond," and there was no need for a new contract after the testing period.

During the three-month trial period, Frank discovered a flaw in the garnet distribution tube. Keith quickly responded by replacing the tube, giving Frank the impression that the flaw had been fixed by the engineering department. Several months after the three-month trial period ended, Frank called Keith to inform him that the garnet distribution tube was malfunctioning again. "I thought you said the tube was redesigned by your engineers," Frank stated, somewhat frustrated. "Not exactly," replied Keith. "What do you mean, not exactly?" Frank shouted. "Look, don't get all worked up," Keith replied, his own emotions beginning to rise. "I'll replace the tube at our own expense." Frank shouted, "I don't want another flawed tube. I want a cutter that can handle my workload. If this damn machine can't do it, I want my money back!" Keith figured he had had enough of Frank's abusive language.

He replied calmly, "Read the specs sheet, the warranty, and the sales agreement you signed at the beginning of the three-month trial period. We have lived up to everything in that agreement." Frank shouted, "Except I have a piece of equipment that you promised was reengineered. I have no interest in replacing a garnet tube every four months." At this point Keith was at a loss, since his engineering department was working on correcting the flawed tube, but had not yet found a solution. Their dispute ended in a lawsuit filed by Frank.

The situation between Frank and Keith is becoming more commonplace as new technology is generated at an accelerated rate. In the face of fierce competition and shorter turnover times, new technology is not as thoroughly tested as in the past. The customer is more commonly used as the test vehicle on the assumption that the problems encountered can be quickly and economically corrected. New information technology and software are prime examples of this situation.

Suppose Keith and Frank had a provider-customer relationship where they were both committed to each others' mutual success. In this relationship both parties could be truthful. Both parties could mutually share their problems and correspondingly, the power of a solution. This is a new relationship between provider and customer, but one we believe necessary to address the accelerated rate of research, development, and business application.

Oh, by the way, what happened with Frank's lawsuit? The president of Keith's company, Ravi Singh, brought Keith and Frank together to "revisit" the sequence of events leading to the lawsuit filed by Frank. Ravi listened carefully to Frank's frustration with their new water-jet cutter. He also astutely sensed Frank's anxiety in being able to meet the increasing demands of his business.

After listening carefully to Frank's concerns, Ravi informed Frank that they had not yet solved the problem of the flawed garnet tube—but that they were close to a solution. He proposed they work together in correcting the flaw in the garnet tube design, provide free replacement tubes as needed until a solution was found, and renegotiate the contractual agreement to both their satisfaction. Frank was satisfied with Ravi's proposal, and he subsequently dropped the suit.

The breakthrough in this situation was telling the truth about the garnet tube. The truth always establishes the basis for a breakthrough in relationship—whether it's business or personal. Problems are much easier to solve when an open, honest, and mutually supportive relationship exists between provider and customer.

Conclusion

The essence of customer service is an unconditional commitment to the customer's success, growth, and well-being. Success means doing everything in our power, including fulfilling "unreasonable" requests, to exceed their expectations. Growth involves sharing ideas, best practices, and how a customer might establish more empowering relationships with his or her employees as an external observer. Customer well-being involves sharing insights and personal experiences, where appropriate, of how a customer might attain his or her own physical, mental, and emotional well-being—particularly where excessive stress and work demands are involved. All three of these dimensions ultimately lead to a "customer for life"—if not in a business capacity, then in an enduring personal relationship.

The Rules *for* Success

Our real destination has been to discover, through experiential learning, *The Rules for Success*. Based upon our learning journey through the hazards of failure, we have *naturally* discovered the following Rules for Success.

Rule #1: *Continuous Learning* means adopting a mind-set of self-motivated learning because it's fun, exciting, and ultimately a necessity for navigating life— personally and professionally. Continuous learning is the essence of a Learning Organization.

Rule #2: *Knowledge Sharing* means the proactive habit of comprehensively disseminating new insights, ideas, or nuggets of wisdom to all those who comprise your personal or professional network. Knowledge sharing establishes the basis for future collaboration ventures that enhance your career that you could never predict in advance.

Rule #3: *Quality Relationships* are the fundamental basis of any joint activity that is based upon honesty, integrity, and trust. It is the interpersonal glue that holds any human endeavor together through difficulties and trying times on the road to success.

Rule #4: *Win/Win* means that any joint effort based upon honesty, integrity, and trust will, by definition, result in value and success for everyone involved. It begins with a natural intent to ensure the success of others; and in doing so, ensure one's own success.

Rule #5: *Share the Wealth* means there is enough for everyone; in terms of money, awards, recognition, or whatever one is driven to acquire. One's own success and well-being is ultimately measured by the success and well-being of everyone involved in a project or venture. It is the recognition that wealth comes in many forms: money, resources, kindness, and love.

Rule #6: *Responsibility* means the willingness to view yourself as the *principal source* of what happens in your life. It is a cognitive skill that takes into account everything that could possibly happen *before* a project, an activity, or a undertaking is put into action. Responsibility drives intention to "make it happen" no matter what it takes for success.

Rule #7: *Accountability* means the willingness to *own* the results that occur in your life—irrespective of reasons or excuses. It also means "if I participated in something, then I own what happened." This way of thinking leads to proactive action to learn from what did not work, as well as to find solutions, rather than find fault in others.

Rule #8: *Integrity* means being true to yourself and others. It includes both *honesty* and *truth* in not only what you say but also in what you do. It also defines your character in terms of your ability to influence others—which we define as leadership.

Rule #9: *Exceed Expectations* means to go beyond what's expected to be successful in life. Exceeding expectations puts you in a class alone. Whether you succeed or not (and you probably will) you have measurably increased your value and probability of success for anything you desire.

Rule #10: *Customer Service* means the recognition that we are employed because of the existence of a customer—internal and/or external. Customer service requires the experience of humility in putting the needs of someone else first, in preference to one's self.

Acknowledgements

We would like to acknowledge and thank all of those who contributed their personal stories included in this book. In many cases, we took the liberty to "embellish" the stories in order to add humor or a bit of "tongue in cheek." In spite of these liberties, the essence of all the stories has been retained. We also acknowledge, with appreciation, those who read the manuscript and made valuable suggestions during the writing: Barbara Thompson, Sue Kwon, Mutiu Fagbayi, Ulla Knoll, Lea and Kayla Guillory, Shauna Black, Connie Howard, Diana Derval, and Brenda Rogers. Finally, we gratefully acknowledge Becky Harding who initally edited the book, Kathleen Di Francesco who designed the cover, Tatiana Haynes who designed the inside pages, and Trish Withus who edited the final contents.

Bill and Phil
April 2009

About The Authors

Bill Guillory

William A. Guillory, Ph.D., is the President and founder of Innovations Consulting International, Inc. He has presented more than 4,000 seminars throughout corporate America, Europe, Asia Pacific, Mexico, Middle East, and Canada. He has facilitated seminars for over 300 corporations, including the senior management of American Airlines, Amgen, Inc., Eastman Kodak Company, Electronic Data Systems, Lockheed Martin Corporation, Brambles Corporation of Australia, TDIndustries, Texas Instruments, Sempra Energy, DaimlerChrysler, Kellogg Corporation, Providence Health System, Duke University Health System, and many other Fortune 500 corporations.

Dr. Guillory is an authority on diversity, empowerment, leadership, creativity, and work-life quality and balance. He is a widely requested conference and keynote speaker on these subjects as well as spirituality in the workplace. He is the author of four books on personal transformation, "Realizations," "It's All an Illusion," "Destined to Succeed," and "The Guides," and is the co-author of the popular management book titled "EMPOWERMENT For High-Performing Organizations." His most recent books are "Spirituality in the Workplace," "The FuturePerfect Organization," and "Animal Kingdom—A Diversity Fable."

Prior to establishing Innovations, Dr. Guillory was a physical chemist of international renown. His distinguished awards and appointments include an Alfred P. Sloan Fellowship, an Alexander von Humboldt appointment at the University of Frankfurt, a Ralph Metcalf Chair at Marquette University, and the Chancellor's Distinguished

Lectureship at the University of California at Berkeley. Dr. Guillory founded Innovations in 1985 following a period of intense personal growth which led to a career change to personal and organizational transformation.

Phil Davis

Phil Davis is president and CEO of ZDocs, a company that helps large organizations and independent authors publish books and other information. Prior to starting ZDocs, Phil and his family lived in Japan for 12 years while he served as VP of Operations of Asia Pacific for two U.S. companies, Flow International and Kinko's International. Phil graduated from Brigham Young University with a degree in Accounting and minor degrees in Economics and English.

While most of his time is spent helping others publish and promote their books, Phil is the author of *Fast & Furious Book Promotion*: a system for promoting books online. His websites include, www.howtopublishabookblog.com, www.authorsonthenet.com, and www.zdocsonline.com.

Innovations International, Inc.

Innovations is a global human resource development corporation specializing in personal and organizational transformation. We exist to assist organizations in achieving their business performance goals while maintaining their personal and collective well-being.

Our areas of expertise include:

- Diversity
- Empowerment
- Leadership
- Creativity and Innovation
- Work-Life Integration
- Quantum-Thinking
- High-Performance Management Systems
- Spirituality in the Workplace

Our most recent offerings include *Leading in the 21st Century—The FuturePerfect Organization, Virtual Collaboration—The Intersection of Information Technology and Human Dynamics*, and *Quantum Thinking—Higher Order Creativity and Innovation.* Comprehensive discussions of these specializations are on the websites www.where-to-now.com and www.innovint.com.

These areas of expertise include comprehensive programs involving consulting, seminars, audits and assessments, executive coaching, strategic planning, and interactive multimedia learning.

Our multimedia and online series in Diversity and High Performance feature CD-ROM interactive programs including video presentations and scenarios, question-and-answer discussions, interactive case studies, and self-management skills.

For information regarding Innovations' programs, telephone, write, fax, email, or visit our website:

Innovations International, Inc.
5442 South 900 East, Suite 551
Salt Lake City, UT 84117 USA
Tel: (800) 693-3594 Fax: (800) 693-9430
Email: innovations@innovint.com
Website: www.innovint.com

ZDocs, Inc.

ZDocs specializes in helping both corporations and individuals publish and promote books and other documents. With state-of-the art digital printing equipment, we offer a true just-in-time delivery system that helps customers reduce costs. In addition, just-in-time delivery gives our customers the flexibility to print in small runs, make changes to their documents and then go to print again.

For medium to large corporations, we offer a turnkey fulfillment solution. Our fulfillment center brings all the components of a customer's kit – books, postcards, brochures, CDs, etc. – into our warehouse to be picked, packed, and shipped. This solution works great for companies running a seminar operation.

For independent authors, we offer a front-end package that helps authors choose the best way to publish their book, how to build a promotional plan and how to use the Internet to promote their book to the world. This is a web-based service called Authors On The Net (www.authorsonthenet.com).

ZDocs, Inc.
81 South 1380 West
Lindon, UT 84042
Toll Free: (866) 669-3627
Email: zdocs@zdocsonline.com
www.zdocsonline.com

Other Titles by William A. Guillory

Realizations

The Business of Diversity

The Global Manager

It's All an Illusion

EMPOWERMENT for High-Performing Organizations

Destined to Succeed

The Guides

Rodney—The Children's Series

Rodney Goes to the Country— The Children's Series

The Living Organization— Spirituality in the Workplace

Living Without Fear

Tick Tock!...Who Broke the Clock?

The FuturePerfect Organization— Driven by Quantum Leadership

Animal Kingdom —A Diversity Fable

ORDER FORM

How To Become A Total Failure —
The Ten Rules of Highly Unsuccessful People

1-99 copies	at 9.95 each
100-499 copies	at 7.95 each
500-999 copies	at 7.00 each
1000 or more copies	at 6.95 each

> To place orders, call toll free **800-693-3594** or drop
> your order in the mail using this order form.
> Orders may be faxed to **800-693-9430**

Name _____

Job Title _____

Organization _____

Phone _____ Email _____

Street Address _____

P.O. Box _____ Zip _____

City, State_____ Zip _____

Country_____

Purchase Order Number (If applicable) _____

Applicable sales tax, shipping and handling charges will be added.
Prices subject to change.
Orders less than $500 require prepayment. $500 or more may be invoiced.

☐ Check Enclosed   ☐ Please Invoice

☐ VISA   ☐ Master Card   ☐ American Express

Account Number _____ Expiration Date _____

Signature_____

800-693-3594
Overnight or Second Day Deliveries
Available via FedEx or UPS